THE SECRET CHIEF REVEALED

Conversations with Leo Zeff, a Pioneer in the Underground Psychedelic Therapy Movement

MYRON J. STOLAROFF

Featuring Stanislav Grof, Albert Hofmann, and Ann & Alexander 'Sasha' Shulgin

MULTIDISCIPLINARY ASSOCIATION FOR PSYCHEDELIC STUDIES

Co-published by Synergetic Press & the Multidisciplinary Association for Psychedelic Studies (MAPS)

ISBN 9780966001969 (paperback)
ISBN 9781737092469 (ebook)

Revised Ed. editorial, cover & book design by Synergetic Press
1st & 2nd Ed. Project Editor: Rick Doblin
1st & 2nd Ed. Manuscript Editors: Sylvia Thyssen and Brandy Doyle
Additional editing help from Jon Hanna and Valerie Mojeiko
Photos: Jack Coddington
Printed in the USA

TABLE OF CONTENTS

This book is dedicated to
the memory of Leo,
with the fervent hope
that the revelation
of his work
will help bring
understanding and sanity
to a confused world.
May it pave the way
for others to reap the benefits
he worked so hard
to establish.

ACKNOWLEDGMENTS

I WISH TO EXPRESS my thanks to a number of persons who helped to make this book possible.

First, I wish to thank Leo, wherever he may be, for his devoted interest, skill, and determination in carrying out this very important work under stressful conditions, guided by his faith and confidence in the value of what he was doing. My wife Jean and I are most grateful for the patience and care that he took to communicate to us his knowledge and experience.

I am also grateful to those who participated in Leo's program, making this work possible, and particularly to those who shared in detail the experiences that they underwent and the results that followed. I also thank Leo's family and supporters who aided him in carrying out his work.

I wish to thank Ann and Sasha Shulgin for pointing out to me the importance of getting Jacob's efforts recorded.

My thanks to Terence McKenna for permission to use his title for this book.

I am extremely indebted to Rick Doblin, Sylvia Thyssen, Brandy Doyle and MAPS for their assistance in the editing and completion of the manuscript, and for taking the steps to have the manuscript published.

I wish to thank my wife Jean for her assistance and loving support throughout all stages of this project, from the initial interviews to the completion of the final manuscript.

INTRODUCTION TO THE SECOND EDITION

THE SECRET CHIEF REVEALED was published seven years ago, and has now been sold out. Reprinting a new edition provides the opportunity to make some fresh observations, as well as report new progress in the utilization of psychedelic substances. Moreover, the passage of time permits a new development: The Secret Chief no longer needs to be kept secret!

While doing his important work, which our government held to be illegal, Leo lived constantly under the possibility of being discovered and prosecuted as a criminal. Many of those close to Leo who supported his work also lived under the threat of exposure. Even family members feared harassment or investigation. Leo died over seventeen years ago, and the threat to his supporters and companions has evaporated. His family members no longer object to the revealing of his name, and share in the belief that it is time for Leo to receive the acknowledgment he deserves. So we are pleased to present Leo Zeff, Ph.D., the Secret Chief! In this edition, we include photographs of Leo and new accounts written by his son and daughter, as well as new reports taken from interviews with his clients.

Since the last edition, we have new reasons to hope that the healing techniques Leo pioneered may reach more people. Most promising is the action of the FDA in approving three projects investigating the efficacy of psychedelics as tools for therapy, the first such action in over thirty years. In addition, a number of new, informative books help clear up widespread misunderstanding of the nature and potential of psychedelics.

It has now been 24 years since my wife Jean and I interviewed Leo. What a marvelous experience this was for the both of us! Leo was a remarkable friend, full of life and wisdom and good cheer. It was a true joy to spend many hours with him as he reviewed his work with us. Turning my attention to once again consider his contribution, I feel a deep emptiness in his absence. And yet as I look over what he shared, I cannot help but be immensely grateful for his outstanding contribution.

Still, I am saddened at how a most priceless gift, the psychedelic substances, especially in the hands of Leo and others like him, has been completely denigrated by our government. The enormous potential for healing, for self-discovery, and for communion with the Divine has been prohibited. Those who would pursue such valuable goals can do so only by becoming criminals, as our current laws forbid possession of such substances.

But there is hope. There is a deepening spirituality growing in our nation, and spirituality is a powerful aid to healing. Many extremely worthwhile books are appearing. Some of these pertaining specifically to how psychedelics can help have been added to the "Resources" section at the end of this book. And as mentioned above, the FDA has approved three projects authorizing research with psychedelic substances to evaluate their effectiveness for therapy. One project involves the application of psilocybin in the treatment of Obsessive Compulsive Disorder. Another is employing MDMA in the treatment of Posttraumatic Stress Disorder (PTSD), and a third employs psilocybin administered to advanced cancer patients to relieve anxiety, pain, and fear of death. These projects have evolved as a result of anecdotal evidence from underground therapists and users, as well as from previous psychedelic research from thirty years ago. Successful outcomes from these three projects could well open the door to more extensive research.

In the meantime, it would be most helpful if government officials and the public were better informed of the remarkable potential that psychedelics hold for healing, learning, self-development, and authentic spiritual understanding. In general, the DEA and government agencies have feared widespread abuse and damage from such substances. It is true that uninformed or misdirected use of psychedelics can be harmful. The government must certainly take some responsibility for this situation, as criminalizing these substances has prevented important knowledge for harm reduction and beneficial uses to be made available. However, for a realistic evaluation of the risks, a number of issues should be taken into account:

1. There are large numbers of users who have learned to use psychedelics properly for their own personal gain, encompassing the range from increased enjoyment or improved functioning to the heights of spiritual development. Many knowledgeable therapists are willing to break

the law rather than withhold valuable treatments with these substances from their clients.

2. A minor percentage of the population are at risk of developing unhealthy relationships with psychedelics due to personality disorders or other pre-existing psychological conditions. They are often incapable of comprehending the consequences of their actions, including abusing drugs. This minority will always be a problem until we devise better ways to care for them.

3. A fairly large percentage of young people live in painful circumstances—in poverty-stricken, abusive, or neglectful families. The unhappiness of such youngsters lead them to explore almost any avenue that will provide them with a period of enjoyment, regardless of the circumstances or aftermath. Prohibition, however, will not solve the problems faced by these young people. In fact, legalization would make vital information more available, and knowledgeable guides would begin to appear, which in time would reduce misuse.

4. The use of psychedelics is self-regulating in most cases. Their true purpose is to enhance growth and interior development. Used only for pleasure, or abused, the Inner Self is thwarted, which leads to unpleasant experiences and depression. Though everyone who pursues the use of psychedelics for personal growth must be prepared for the "dark night of the soul" experiences, those who seek only entertainment will lose interest in these substances. A good example comes from the book The Pursuit of Ecstasy, by Jerome Beck and Marsha Rosenbaum, which reports on a study funded by the National Institute of Drug Abuse (NIDA). "Chapter 5, Limits to Use: Why People Moderate or Quit Ecstasy," covers a number of factors why people reduce or drop their use of Ecstasy (MDMA) over time, based on a large sample of interviews conducted with a broad spectrum of users. It must be recognized that despite the action of our government to make psychedelic substances illegal, huge numbers of people have found psychedelics so useful that they are willing to break the law in order to use them. It is hoped that such users can obtain valuable information from this book that will reduce abuse and promote true healing, growth, and wisdom. The combination of

successful research results and the growth in public recognition of the vital role of psychedelics in healing and personal development should ultimately restore these enormously valuable tools to our society. Then the dedicated pioneering work of Leo Zeff will be fully recognized and appreciated.

PROLOGUE

STANISLAV GROF

AFTER THE PUBLICATION of the first clinical paper on LSD by Walter A. Stoll in 1947, Albert Hofmann's serendipitous discovery of the psychedelic effects of LSD became practically an overnight sensation in the world of science. Never before had a single substance held so much promise in such a wide variety of fields of interest.

For neuropharmacologists and neurophysiologists, the discovery of LSD meant the beginning of a golden era of research that could solve many puzzles concerning the intricate biochemical interactions underlying the functioning of the brain.

Experimental psychiatrists saw this substance as a unique means for creating a laboratory model for naturally occurring psychoses, particularly schizophrenia. They hoped that it could provide unparalleled insights into the nature of these mysterious disorders and open new avenues for their treatment.

LSD was also highly recommended as a unique teaching device that would make it possible for clinical psychiatrists and psychologists to spend a few hours in the world of their patients and as a result of it to understand them better, be able to communicate with them more effectively, and improve their ability to help them.

Early experiments with LSD revealed its unique potential as a powerful tool offering the possibility of deepening and accelerating the psychotherapeutic process, as well as extending the range of applicability of psychotherapy to categories of patients that previously had been difficult to reach such as alcoholics, narcotic drug addicts, and criminal recidivists.

Particularly valuable and promising were the early efforts to use LSD psychotherapy with terminal cancer patients. These studies showed that

LSD was able to relieve severe pain, often even in those patients who had not responded to medication with narcotics. In a large percentage of these patients, it was also possible to alleviate or even eliminate the fear of death, increase the quality of their lives during the remaining days, and positively transform the experience of dying.

For the historians and critics of art, the LSD experiments provided extraordinary new insights into the psychology and psychopathology of art, particularly various modern movements as well as paintings and sculptures of native cultures.

The spiritual experiences frequently observed in LSD sessions offered a radically new understanding of a wide variety of phenomena from the world of religion, including shamanism, the rites of passage, the ancient mysteries of death and rebirth, the Eastern spiritual philosophies, and the mystical traditions of the world.

LSD research seemed to be well on its way to fulfilling all the above promises and expectations when it was suddenly interrupted by unsupervised mass experimentation of the young generation and the ensuing repressive measures of a legal, administrative, and political nature.

However, the problems associated with this development, blown out of proportion by sensation-hunting journalists, were not the only reason why LSD and other psychedelics were rejected by the Euro-American culture. An important contributing factor was also the attitude of technologized societies toward non-ordinary states of consciousness.

All ancient and pre-industrial societies held these states in high esteem and they devoted much time and energy trying to develop safe and effective ways of inducing them. Members of these social groups had the opportunity to repeatedly experience non-ordinary states in a variety of sacred and secular contexts.

Because of their capacity to provide experiential access to the numinous dimensions of existence and to the world of archetypal realms and beings, non-ordinary states represented the main vehicle of the ritual and spiritual life of the pre-industrial era. They also played an essential role in the diagnosing and healing of various disorders and were used for cultivation of intuition and extrasensory perception.

By comparison, industrial civilization has pathologized non-ordinary states, developed effective means of suppressing them when they occur spontaneously, and has rejected or even outlawed the contexts and tools that can facilitate them. Because of the resulting naivete and ignorance concerning non-ordinary states, Western culture was unprepared to accept and incorporate the extraordinary mind-altering properties and power of psychedelics.

The sudden invasion of the Dionysian elements from the depths of the unconscious and the heights of the superconscious was too threatening for the Puritanical values of our society. In addition, the irrational and transrational nature of psychedelic experiences seriously challenged the very foundations of the worldview of Western materialistic science. The existence and nature of these experiences could not be explained in the context of the mainstream theories and seriously undermined the metaphysical assumptions on which Western culture is built.

For most psychiatrists and psychologists, psychotherapy meant disciplined discussions or free-associating on the couch. The intense emotions and dramatic physical manifestations in psychedelic sessions appeared to them to be too close to what they were used to considering to be psychopathology. It was hard for them to imagine that such states could be healing and transformative and they did not trust the reports about the extraordinary power of psychedelic psychotherapy.

In addition, many of the phenomena occurring in psychedelic sessions could not be understood within the context of theories dominating academic thinking. The possibilities of reliving birth or episodes from embryonal life, obtaining accurate information from the collective unconscious, experiencing archetypal realities and karmic memories, or perceiving remote events in out-of-body states, were simply too fantastic to be believable for an average professional.

Yet those of us who had the chance to work with psychedelics and were willing to radically change our theoretical understanding of the psyche and practical strategy of therapy were able to see and appreciate the enormous potential of psychedelics, both as therapeutic tools and as substances of extraordinary heuristic value.

In one of my early books, I suggested that the potential significance of LSD and other psychedelics for psychiatry and psychology was comparable to the value the microscope has for biology and medicine or the telescope has for astronomy. My later experience with psychedelics only confirmed this initial impression. These substances function as unspecific amplifiers that increase the energetic niveau in the psyche and make the deep unconscious dynamics available for conscious processing.

This unique property of psychedelics makes it possible to study psychological undercurrents that govern our experiences and behaviors to a depth that cannot be matched by any other methods and tools available in modern mainstream science. In addition, psychedelics offer unique opportunities for healing of emotional and psychosomatic disorders, for positive personality transformation, and consciousness evolution.

Naturally, tools of this power carry with them greater potential risks than more conservative and far less effective tools currently accepted and used by mainstream psychiatry, such as verbal psychotherapy or tranquilizing medication. However, past research has shown that these risks can be minimized through responsible use and careful control of the set and setting.

The legal and administrative sanctions against psychedelics did not deter lay experimentation, but they did terminate all legitimate scientific research of these substances. For those of us who had the privilege to explore the extraordinary potential of psychedelics, this was a tragic loss for psychiatry, psychology, and psychotherapy.

These unfortunate developments wasted what was probably the single most important opportunity in the history of these disciplines. Had it been possible to avoid the unnecessary mass hysteria and continue responsible research of psychedelics, they could have become a tool that would make it possible to radically revise the theory and practice of psychiatry. This research would have brought a new understanding of the psyche and of consciousness that could become an integral part of a comprehensive new scientific paradigm of the twenty-first century.

Most of the LSD researchers grudgingly accepted the legal and political sanctions against psychedelics and reluctantly returned to mainstream therapeutic practices. A few attempted to develop non-drug methods for inducing non-ordinary states of consciousness with the experiential spectrum and healing potential comparable to psychedelics. And then there were those who, like Jacob, the "Secret Chief," refused to accept legal sanctions that they considered irrational, unjustified, or even unconstitutional.

These researchers saw the extraordinary benefits that LSD therapy offered to their clients and decided not to sacrifice the well-being of these people to scientifically unsubstantiated legislation. In addition to the therapeutic value of psychedelics, they were also aware of the entheogenic potential of these substances—their capacity to induce profound spiritual experiences. For this reason, they understood their work with LSD to be not only therapeutic practice, but also religious activity in the best sense of the word. From this perspective, the legal sanctions against psychedelics appeared to be not only unfounded and misguided, but also represented a serious infringement of religious freedom.

Jacob painfully weighed the pros and cons and made the decision to challenge the law, continue his work with psychedelics, and assume personal responsibility for his activity. He has already passed the judgment of his "family," the friends and clients whose lives he has profoundly changed. They remember him with great love and gratitude. It remains to be seen how he will be judged by history. It is certainly wise to obey the laws if our primary concern is personal safety and comfort. However, it often happens that in retrospect, history places higher value on those individuals who violated questionable laws of their time because of foresight and high moral principles than those who had issued them for wrong reasons.

TRIBUTE TO JACOB

ANN SHULGIN

I FIRST MET JACOB, the man who is the subject of *The Secret Chief*—I called him Adam Fisher in *PIHKAL*—in the early 1980s, shortly after I met Sasha Shulgin. One of the great stories I heard from Sasha was about this wonderful psychologist who had—for many years—been guiding certain carefully selected clients through psychedelic sessions. In the early 1970s, this elderly gentleman decided to retire from his regular clinical practice. A chemist friend of Sasha's had, at that time, just rediscovered a drug which had been sitting on a German chemical company shelf, so to speak, since its synthesis in 1912. She had tried it and reported interesting effects to Sasha, who went into his own lab and made the drug, 3,4-methylenedioxymethamphetamine (known as MDMA) and tried the result himself. He called Jacob and told him there was a new drug that might be of interest to him, and shortly afterwards, took it over to Jacob's little apartment.

The rest, as the saying goes, is history. Jacob postponed his retirement, completely enraptured by the effects of MDMA on himself and his patients. Over the next few years, he traveled around the country, quietly training groups of therapists in the use of MDMA in psychotherapy. He occasionally went to Europe to continue this work among European psychologists and psychiatrists. He always insisted that any therapist who intended to make use of this magic drug had to try it themselves first. That has been the rule ever since, whenever healers wish to make use of either MDMA—which is technically not a psychedelic drug—or any of the true psychedelics in their therapy. The therapists *must* know the effects of any such drugs in themselves before giving them to anyone else.

At his memorial, I asked one of his oldest friends whether she had any idea as to how many people Jacob might have initiated over the years in the use of psychedelics, and she replied, "Oh, I would guess about four thousand, give or take a few." Rather extraordinary, for a man in his seventies!

Jacob himself, when I knew him, was everybody's idea of what a grandfather should be. His thinning hair was silvery white. He had a slightly rounded face, and the years had etched into it indelible proof of kindness and humor. One look, and you would instantly trust him to listen and empathize. He was quite capable of anger and stern judgment, but these were reserved for very few people. Malice disturbed him—as it does most of us—but the only time I heard him speak with absolute disgust was when he explained the meaning of what he called the "bear-trapper." That was his term for borderline personality. I suspect he'd been badly burned by at least one in his career as a clinical psychologist.

When I was very young, first hearing and reading about psychology, the worst possible diagnosis used to be something called "inadequate personality." Many of us would have preferred to be diagnosed as paranoid schizophrenic! At least there could be a smidgen of tragic drama attached to paranoia and/or schizophrenia, but to be thought of as an "inadequate personality?" Total horror. These days, the most dreaded diagnosis (speaking of non-violent, non-psychotic patients) is "borderline," and Jacob used the term, "bear-trapper," because, as he explained it, such patients usually try to draw their therapists into their own world, instead of using whatever help the therapist offers. Their goal, as he saw it, is not to gain health, but to seduce the therapist into keeping them company in their state of sickness. They are highly manipulative and, if confronted directly, can become vengeful and destructive. When I first met Jacob, I had not yet begun to do my own work as a psychedelic therapist, and didn't fully understand what he meant by "bear-trapper." I believe that the official definition of such a hapless soul is something like, "Help-refusing complainer," which covers a lot of ground in a very few words. Not too many years later, I began learning how to do therapy with MDMA and psychedelics, and ran into two examples of what Jacob had warned me about. As a result, I finally understood my dear friend's allergy to such people, although I was never sufficiently burned myself to develop the kind of anger Jacob had expressed towards them.

Jacob was not a brilliant genius, but he was one of the people from whom

I learned most about what is called "wisdom," because that is what he had. He could take a situation which would ordinarily cause high frustration or anxiety in anybody else and turn it into a wonderfully palatable spiritual lesson, seasoned with great humor and joy.

When you asked Jacob a meaningful question, his answer tended to give you the maximum amount of useful information in the least number of words. And he had learned not to be defensive about making mistakes. In fact, I never saw Jacob being defensive about anything; he was at peace with himself and comfortable with who he was, which is certainly one of the definitions of a good healer.

I described, in *PIHKAL*, Jacob's role in helping me through a strange and extraordinary week of consciousness change which happened many years ago. It was his words, "What you're going through is a process. All you have to do is not get in its way," that gave me my bearings and enabled me to regard the entire experience as a chance to learn and grow, which is exactly what it became.

The strangest thing about Jacob, for many of us, was the fact that, as a young man, he had been in the United States Army and loved it. He was amused by the bewilderment of so many of his friends who couldn't quite understand how a deeply committed psychedelic guide and therapist could regard past duty in the military as a productive and enjoyable experience. Most of us eventually realized that the problem was in our own prejudices and projections, not in Jacob's validation of both worlds. I asked him once whether he thought there was any hope for survival of our species, considering the apparent determination of so many of us to poison our environment and destroy each other. He turned to me, smiling, "I think we'll make it. Humanity has a funny way of turning itself around when it has to. Maybe not all of us will survive, but I have no doubt at all that our species will. It's happened many times before; it will again."

We miss Jacob. That old cliche, "It is a privilege to have known him," is absolutely appropriate, for Sasha and me and for all of his friends. The only thing I can't forgive him for is that he left this plane, this reality that he shared with us, without my knowing in time. I wasn't there, by his bedside, and it still grieves me when I think about it. One of these days, one of these years, I will be able to give him permission—from my heart—to go, but I haven't been able to do it yet.

FOREWORD

ALBERT HOFMANN

HARDLY ANY OTHER SCIENCE as conservative and tradition-bound as is medicine. Whenever a new treatment modality or an extraordinary medicine appears, in addition to interested acceptance in specialist circles there is also opposition to the novelty, which is emotional and vehement, in proportion as the innovation is significant and pioneering. Hypnosis may be cited as an example. It was denounced as dangerous charlatanism, and more than a century had to pass before it gained entry into mainstream medicine.

Today a novel group of psychoactive substances, which have come to be known under various designations—hallucinogens, psychotomimetics, psychedelics, and entheogens—has evoked violent controversy in professional circles and the media. These are substances capable of profoundly affecting human consciousness. This explains the vehemence and the passion which accompany discussions of the 'psychedelics,' as these materials are mostly known today, since we are talking about the veritable inner core of our humanity, our consciousness.

On the other hand, one would imagine that psychedelics might have gained especially easy entry into medicinal practice, since we are dealing here with active principles of drugs which for millennia have played a meaningful role in archaic cultures and which even today among primigenial peoples find beneficent application in social and medicinal fields. Had we from the outset harked back to these archaic experiences, we would have been able to avoid the misuse and improper use of these extremely potent psychopharmaceuticals, and they would not now be prohibited, but would rather have become valuable medicines in the contemporary pharmacopoeia.

The substances under discussion are above all mescaline, the active agent of a Mexican cactus which the Indians call *peyotl* or peyote; psilocybin, the active principle of the Mexican 'magic mushrooms' *teonandcatl*; and LSD (chemically *Lysergsaure diathylamid* or lysergic acid diethylamide), which is closely related to lysergic acid hydroxyethylamide, the active agent of the ancient Indian 'magic drug' *ololiuhqui.*

All of these drugs are integrated into tribal cultures and employed as 'magic medicines' in a religious-ceremonial context. Their use is in the hands of shamans or shamanesses, male or female priest-doctors, where they manifest a beneficent action. They are esteemed as sacred, and according to Indian belief, their misuse or profanation is punished by the gods with insanity or death.

International research with these substances—especially in psychiatry, to investigate their use as pharmacological adjuncts to psychoanalysis and psychotherapy—commenced shortly after the 1943 discovery of LSD, which is by far the most potent representative of the psychedelics. Besides the greatest enthusiasm in response to outstanding results with LSD and other psychedelics, skepticism also manifested itself in conservative circles, particularly those in which any pharmacological intervention in the treatment process was rejected.

This very promising use of psychedelics in psychiatry and psychology came to an untimely end midway through the sixties, when this new class of pharmaceuticals was outlawed, with the complete prohibition of their manufacture, possession, and use. Accidents involving psychedelics resulting from frivolous, uncontrolled use in the drug scene were the ostensible reason for this prohibition. The principal reason for the draconian prohibitive measures, however, was the goal of attacking the youth movement, hippies and the like, who opposed the Establishment and the Vietnam War, and whose 'cult-drug' was, above all, LSD.

Medicinal use of psychedelics was prevented by the official prohibition, and further research in this field was interrupted while consumption continued in the drug scene. This irrational situation still largely exists today.[1] For therapists, the use of psychedelics became a criminal matter, for which they could face punishment.

One of the very few therapists who continued to use psychedelics, accepting the great risk of criminality, was the psychologist here referred to by the alias 'Jacob' and dubbed the 'Secret Chief.'[2]

Jacob had obtained mostly excellent results from his specially developed techniques in the use of psychedelics, and he realized that this therapeutic method should not be withheld from sick people. His ethical obligation as a therapist, to help people took priority for him over obedience to a dubious official prohibition.

In the illegality of his time, it was unthinkable to publish the excellent results of his therapy. It is therefore praiseworthy that today, nine years after his death, a friend has undertaken the task of publishing the details of the therapeutic methodology of this intrepid Ph.D. psychologist. The therapeutic results attained from this method constitute an important argument in the current growing discussion challenging medical circles, whether again to liberate psychedelics for psychotherapeutic practice.[3]

[1] On the other hand, some very limited psychedelic research was permitted to begin again in 1990.- Ed.

[2] Jacob was nicknamed the "Secret Chief" by Terence McKenna.- Ed.

[3] This foreword was translated from German by Jonathan Ott

INTRODUCTION TO THE FIRST EDITION

MYRON J. STOLAROFF

IT IS RARE IN LIFE to meet a person so engaging, so warm, so obviously kind that your heart automatically goes out to him at first contact. Jacob was such a person. Completely unpretentious, he was tremendously enthused with life and excited about people.

Jacob died in the spring of 1988 at the age of 76, after an unusual and illustrious career. He was outstanding in his field, and made many significant contributions. Yet because of the unorthodox character of his chosen work, he was little known outside his immediate circle of friends and clients. In fact, I cannot even use his correct name, nor give you the locale of his activities. Yet if he and his work were truly known, the world would recognize that it has lost one of its most able pioneers and a man who has made a very important contribution to the field of psychology. A close and knowledgeable friend, who had the opportunity to understand him better than most, dubbed him the "Secret Chief," which is a most fitting title for this work.

It was in the spring of 1981 when my wife Jean and I met with him to have these conversations. He was already 70 years old and retired from his very engrossing work. He was a short man, about five feet, six inches tall, somewhat stocky, almost white-haired, and hardly ever to be caught without an engaging smile. As soon as you were in his presence you knew that he was your friend and would do anything he could for you. He was proud of his Jewish heritage, and also proud of his service in the army, where he attained the rank of Lieutenant Colonel.

Jacob was a psychologist, and one of the first to be licensed as a Ph.D. in the state in which he practiced. For many years, he conducted a private practice as a Jungian therapist.

Jacob's life changed dramatically in the early 1960s when he became acquainted with the mind-altering substances, LSD and mescaline. These powerful drugs not only led him into a whole new area of self-understanding, but he found them to be enormously effective in helping his clients—so much so that he abandoned conventional therapy to pursue the study and practice of using these new substances.

Jacob made great personal progress, and at the same time learned a good deal about how to use these chemicals effectively. He developed many useful procedures and had a large following of clients wanting to take advantage of this new, powerful means of therapy. In time, Jacob not only was responsible for processing around three thousand individuals, but he shared his experience in this new art with over one hundred therapists. By the time these conversations were held, he was responsible—probably more than any other individual alive—for introducing individual clients and therapists to the benefits and procedures of effectively using mind-altering substances in personal growth.

My purpose in interviewing Jacob was to become familiar with the practices he had developed. There were many of us who believed that his valuable techniques should be published and made available to other researchers and for posterity. One huge, giant obstacle confronted us: Most such substances had been placed in Schedule I of the Federal government's Controlled Substances Act, making them illegal to possess. So there was considerable risk of exposure in making such information public.

Jacob agreed to transmit the information and have it on record, and we agreed that we would decide later on its disposition. When the information had been reduced to writing, Jacob decided that it was too sensitive to be published, so it was set aside. Now that he is no longer with us, and immune to what ever legal transgressions he may have committed, it becomes possible to tell his story and acknowledge the outstanding pioneering work that he accomplished.

Most of what follows is in Jacob's own words. I have done some editing for the sake of clarity, and have arranged some discussions in more logical progression. Also, appropriate fictitious names and locations have been used with an eye to our repressive drug laws. Many of the very promising substances Jacob worked with are in Schedule I, making it exceedingly difficult to research their beneficial uses.[1]

The decision to use Jacob's own words took much pondering on my part. Several who have seen the initial form of this manuscript felt that Jacob's uninhibited language and looseness of expression would turn many potential readers away, and they preferred a more scholarly, professional rendition. But those who knew Jacob will delight in once more experiencing his expressions, fondly recalling past conversations and the images of this dear person they invoke. Such expressions may likely be lost on readers who never knew this man, and who could very well object to the sometimes coarse language.

But this gets to the very heart of some of the misunderstandings about psychedelics. Jacob was a man who brought new life and opportunity to many hundreds of individuals, often in total life-transforming ways. He was dearly loved. This was not because of his elegant expression or professional training. It was because he was blessed with an abundance of *heart*, the most necessary prerequisite for someone accompanying others into the depths of their very souls. For the unconscious mind is often terribly frightening; we have made much of its contents unconscious because we want nothing to do with it. It takes a strong heart, honesty, and a desire to learn and face one's problems in order to enter the dark areas of our suppressed inner self. Nothing is more helpful than the presence of a kind, loving, and understanding person thoroughly familiar with the dark regions of the mind—a companion who is confident of his ability to help one navigate and resolve those regions that have been an enormous burden in the past, a person who knows the wonder of being free. Whoever understands all of this is certainly not concerned about the person's modes of expression, but is only grateful for the heartfelt support.

And this Jacob expressed in abundance. A person who felt deeply, he understood that expressing such feelings is the most honest way of being

[1] The Drug Enforcement Administration, which initiated the scheduling of practically all psychoactive materials, claims that placing the substances into Schedule I does not preclude research. While there is a procedure for researching Schedule I materials, in practice for almost three decades, virtually no clinical research was permitted on this class of substances. The control is exercised by the Food and Drug Administration, which must grant an IND or Investigational New Drug exemption to permit research. For Schedule I materials, a protocol must be submitted and approved by the FDA. At the time of these interviews, numerous applications for IND's for psychoactive materials had been turned down. Beginning in 1990, there has been a liberalization of this policy. In 1997, there are several research projects with psychedelic substances that have been approved by the FDA and the DEA.

oneself. It is not the choice of words, but the ability to feel deeply and genuinely express one's feelings that make one authentic, and which brings people together in true relationship. Since so many of us are afraid of our feelings, the dark side of our unconscious is replete with feelings we do not dare to feel. Once we learn how to find and express them, we can feel the delight of being fully alive by honestly expressing them. Then we deeply appreciate those who function this way.

So in submitting Jacob in his native tongue, I feel that I avoid the disservice of not fully presenting him. I very much hope that the reader, through encountering Jacob's personal expressions, can more readily discern the heart of one of the truly great persons who have lived on this earth. Yes, it's probably true that a man with a Ph.D. in psychology might have learned to speak more correctly, but once you have the privilege of being in this man's presence, who cares?

May you enjoy this introduction to our good friend and psychedelic guide par excellence, Jacob.

THE SECRET CHIEF REVEALED

CHAPTER I

EARLY BEGINNINGS

JACOB: WHAT I WAS HOPING was that you would be able to prepare questions—I work better in response to a stimulus rather than just talking out of my head.

Myron: How did you first get into the use of psychedelic agents?

Jacob: I think it was in 1961, something like that. One of my former patients called me and said, "Jacob, I want to see you. I want to talk to you about something." I said, "All right." She said, "I want to tell you about an experience I just had. I can't talk to anyone else about it because I don't think they'd understand it." So I said, "Sure. Come on in."

She came in and sat down and told me that she had recently had an LSD trip. She told me about her experience, and I was fascinated by it. She felt that I was the only one who could understand it because I was Jungian. I had training as a Jungian analyst and I was doing Jungian analysis at that time.

Well, I was just amazed at this experience, just flabbergasted, because, my God, here I'd been working over 30 years in various disciplines and studies and meditations and all that kind of stuff and every now and then getting a glimpse of the truth on an experiential level. Here, this gal comes in and tells me she dropped this minute quantity of material and she had a solid day of nothing but all those beautiful peak experiences that people will get out of it, and tremendous insights and many growth things and all that. I was very surprised. Didn't do anything about it, particularly. I asked her some questions, but I knew that there was nothing that you could even question about it. You just listen to it and get what she's saying. I got a contact high from her, though! (He laughs heartily.)

About three or four months later another person, a man whom I had worked with earlier, called me. He said "Jacob, I've got to talk to you. I've got to see you about something." I said, "Fine, come on in." He came in and he sat down and he told me he had just had an LSD experience. Well, he told me about his experience, and it was every bit as spectacular as the other one that I'd heard from the lady. Then I really got interested. Not only that, I wanted to find out how the hell I could get into something like that!

I decided to look into it. I had some friends here, and they were into it and knew a lot about it. I wanted to get some information about this stuff for myself. One of them had Sandoz's annotated bibliography of every article that had come out that had been printed until then, and he let me read it. There was something like 1,000 different references, all phases of psychedelics and a paragraph digest of many of the articles. I read that through from the beginning to the end and was very, very impressed because of the tremendous potential that was pointed out from the material in terms of the experience that people had from it. It was mostly LSD and psilocybin. All the tremendous great things they said about it and what came out of scientific journals.

There were only two or three references to something bad. Those mostly were because somebody gave it to somebody without telling them what it was or under the wrong circumstances. I believe one of them was when they gave it to a nurse in a hospital while she was on duty. She didn't know what was happening. She freaked out and jumped out the window, down about seven stories, something like that, and killed herself.

Then I really got serious about exploring. One of the first things I did was find out who's doing it. One of the first places I found out who was doing it was a place set up for just this purpose. I found that out because one of their staff came to give a talk to some psychologists. He talked about the LSD. I met him; that's the first time I ever met him. We had a talk, and he got to realize that I had a great interest in it. He's the one that told me about their place. I went down to visit them and he showed me around, told me things, and gave me the idea of the setup.

I found out other people who were working with it at that time. We had a meeting of people who were interested in it and did a lot of talking about its potentials, shared experiences that people had and all of that. Then there were a couple of other places that I went where people knew things about it. In fact I went to a meeting where Aldous Huxley spent an evening with us telling us all about it. He had a place for tripping in Mexico, a health resort. I went down there once for a trip with another therapist and her group.

When I was so interested and fascinated by it, someone whom I don't remember anymore said, "Jacob, why don't you try it? Find out what it's all about?" I said, "I'd love to, but I don't know where to get it or who to talk to." He said, "What're you talking about? All these people, any one of them, could give you a trip."

I knew someone who was interested in these materials. I was talking to him and asked him if he knew anyone who was willing to give me a trip. He says yes, he knew where I could get a trip and he told me about a fellow who was doing this work. This guy arranged one for me with him and his wife. So I went over there and had a trip. Didn't have much; didn't take much. I get a full trip out of 100 micrograms of acid. They gave me the acid, and I took it, and in nice circumstances, very pleasant, secure. Then I start to turn on. I lay down on a kind of divan that they have there and we played some music, and as I really started to turn on, they started to turn on.

I remember that the first thing I said was, "Why can't it be like this always?" It was a very deep, emotional trip. He asked me to bring some things along that were important to me, and I brought my Torah. I have my own Torah in its ark. Someplace along the line he was playing Kol Nidre, I think. He laid the Torah across my chest and I immediately went into the lap of God. He and I were One. That was...(feeling strong emotion). I can't remember all the different things. What happened was another thing I said out loud—he copied down what I said out loud—I use tape recordings to catch what people say. I said, "Jacob, if ever again you are frightened you deserve the pain of the fear because you will have forgotten that God is with you and protecting you all the time."

As I was coming down I had some pictures that I brought along—pictures of my family, pictures of my father, my brothers, and my mother. The outstanding experience there was, I looked at pictures of my father and my brothers and myself as I was a little boy, and we all were the same person, all of us. There was no difference between us.

I looked at the picture of my mother that I had there and it came alive and I took hold of her hand and we walked through a forest glade or something like that. And I told her—I can cry again, my God—I told her all the different things that I'd never been able to tell her in my life. Just told her what they were! And she listened to them all, she heard them, she did not respond yet we were communicating beautifully. There were other things that happened on the trip, but now I'm going to stop and go to another point.

The space that I was in at the time that I tripped—I was just in the beginning of the late forties—the 50 year crisis that people have going into the second half of life. I see it more as the time when you really get into the spiritual search. I was pretty damned depressed and pretty well-ridden with anxieties which are characteristic of that stage. I was dissatisfied with myself, dissatisfied with my work as an analyst. While I was aware of the value of the work I was doing, I was more acutely aware of its limitations. Having the people come in once a week—I never did see people more often than once a week, maybe twice a week if they were in a crisis—and talking and talking and having hit the desert space, the dead space of life where nothing's happening. And listening to them talking and talking, trying to get out of it working with dreams and all that and nothing happening, and realizing God damn, Jacob, there's nothing you can do except wait until life comes along and gives them a big kick in the ass and they get going again. Nothing's going to happen from me except to be there to listen and to support them.

Well I was in that kind of a space myself, not knowing what to do, where to go. I could only do what I could do; I tried different solutions, but they didn't work. I read books, I read about spiritual things, about God and all that. I got value from it, but it didn't get me out of where I was, actually.

One of the things on the trip that occurred to me was, Jacob, this is the answer you've been looking for! If something like this can do this to you, then—well, I don't know if I filled it out other than saying well, my God, this can jar people loose, this can break people through, this can do all kinds of things. Look what it's doing for you.

I decided then to explore it much more thoroughly. I wanted more trips, to have more experience, to develop it more. I had to find people who had material, that I could get them to sit with me. I remember being with—oh, he was a physician—he was exploring the materials, and I wanted to try grass. He said all right, come by the house here, and I'll have some grass for you and we'll turn on. Well, I was smoking cigarettes in those days. He laid out some joints for me and told me how to inhale it and hold it and all that and so I started to smoke the grass. I smoked it like cigarettes. I inhaled a big drag, held it in my lungs as long as I could and blew it out, then inhaled another one. I did that through two and a half joints, and this was good stuff.

What happened was I really freaked out. I got paranoid as hell! I was lying down on the couch there after I had finished a piece. The agony of the damned went on and on and on such as can happen. Paranoid as hell! Scared to death of everything. If the phone rang I knew it was the police coming in and there was nothing I could do but just give myself up and all that kind of stuff. It was torture! It was a horrible bummer; I had never had a bummer like that in my life until then.

Myron: Were you alone?

Jacob: No, he was there. Some place, about two to three years into it, he came by and put a dish down by me and I picked up my eye and looked at it. I didn't know what it was. I picked up my eye a couple of years later and looked at it and it was some ice cream, with a spoon. He said, "Have some ice cream, Jacob; go ahead."

I picked it up and I took a spoonful of ice cream. I never tasted such ambrosia in my life! It was the exact opposite experience of what I was having. Heavenly! I ate and ate and ate for I don't know how many years. Every bite was so beautiful! Finally I licked the spoon and I licked the bowl clean. I put it back down, laid back on the couch, and went right back into the bummer!

It took quite a while for me to come down from it, and I did. That was my second trip. I had some other trips that were very nice. I can't remember specifically now. I did have mescaline; that was good, very spiritual, very nice. I took acid some more. Two very interesting and important experiences I had. One was with an experienced psychiatrist, let's call him Louis. Let me see if I can remember what the hell I had then. I think it was an acid trip. I remember I was smoking at that time, I was smoking a pack and a half a day, which is a lot of cigarettes. I was having problems at home with my wife, and was pretty unhappy then in my home life. On this trip I was talking—I was coming down from it, somewhat—and I was talking to Louis about things. He had asked me questions to get me to talk, and I was talking about Jane. I was saying something about the problems that I was having with her. I couldn't talk to her, I couldn't relate to her, she was very frightened about anything that I was doing and very paranoid about me. Very jealous, absolutely no reason of any kind at all. I used to have migraines in the early days, but more than anything else what bothered me the most was the fact that she smoked, constantly. And I'm allergic to cigarette smoke. I was telling him that. I was telling Louis, "See. I can't stand cigarette smoke." Louis looks at me and I'm sitting there with a cigarette in my hand. I say, "I'm allergic to smoke, to cigarette smoke."

He says, "You're allergic to smoke?"

I said, "Yes."

He looks at the cigarette and looks at me, and looks at the cigarette, and I look at the cigarette, too. I'm still pretty stoned. I looked and looked and looked for a long, long, time, I looked at that cigarette. Hours, just looked at it. Many things were going through my mind. Louis says to me, "Well, if you're allergic to cigarettes, are you going to stop smoking?"

After a long pause, I don't know what time it was, but I responded. I said, "That's the wrong question, Louis. The question is not, am I going to quit, the question is, have I quit?" I watched that cigarette burn down to the cork tip in my fingers, and I stuffed it out. And I've never smoked a cigarette since then. I was never able to. I had tried to stop many times, you know how you try to stop. I've never smoked a cigarette since then.

There's another incident, too, an experience in my home that I had that was a very important one. I've had migraines all my life. The earliest memory I have of myself is lying on the front porch of my house at home while they're paving the street and the tar was there as they were paving the street and bricks as they used in those days and the tar smell was making my head ache so bad. That's the earliest experience I had. About three, maybe four years old. The headaches were extremely severe and painful. Pretty bad constantly.

One day I was tripping in a group trip. I was having an ibogaine trip. Do you know ibogaine? It's a fantastic medicine, really. I think I mentioned that we use the word medicine rather than drugs.

You get the answers to all your questions on this trip, on the ibogaine trip. Everything is clearly stated, any questions you have. You go into the trip with questions if you want to. You ask the question but you don't try to answer it. The answer comes to you. This time I decided to ask Mr. Ibogaine—we call him, the person from whom you get the answer, Mr. Ibogaine. Anyway, my question was, what is this with these headaches that I have, that I suffer from? That's all. I was really turned on and deep in a trip and the question occurred to me. Okay, ask it. "What is it with these headaches?"

The answer came. I've had a number of ibogaine trips and the answer always comes. You may not recognize it for what it is, it may be very ambiguous or somewhat like that, but you've got the answer for sure, you'd better hang onto it. The answer came back and said, "You're going to die." I looked, and I said, "What?" That's what it said. I know it said it. I looked around it, and it said I'm going to die.

You don't get frightened with an experience like that. You just take whatever's handed to you and look at it, handle it. So I looked at it, and I looked at it and I said, "Jesus Christ, what does that mean, I'm going to die? Well it means you're going to die, that's all it means." Die when? Of course I knew I'm going to die some day. I know that, that's nothing new. This isn't the kind of "You're going to die" that Mr. Ibogaine was saying.

I said, "Well, gee, this is something between me and Mr. Ibogaine. It is not something that I can tell anybody about." On the report of my trip—we all gathered the next morning and told what happened on our trip—on the report of my trip, I could not say anything to them about Mr. Ibogaine's saying I'm going to die, since that would scare the hell out of everybody. They wouldn't know how to take it.

I didn't know how to take it. I never did know. I kept reflecting on it for quite some time. And it was about a month later. The only relief I could ever get for migraine was codeine. And I took one helluva lot of codeine. I was certainly habituated, but not addicted because there were times I wanted to quit taking it, and I decided I was going to quit. I did quit; I quit for weeks, and I could do it! Without too much trouble. And my migraines would be easier on me even then. But then I'd get back on it again. I was taking as many as four to eight half-grain tablets of codeine every day, so that I could function without the pain.

A month after this trip I took another trip. I don't remember what the material was. It wasn't ibogaine. I was with somebody, I can't remember who it was, I don't even remember if it was a man or a woman. I took something, I think it was acid, and had my trip. As I was coming down from the trip, as most of the people liked to do and as I always wanted to do, I walked down to the water. I walked along the water, which was a very important place for me. That's where I had my greatest conversations with God. That was really a very important thing to me. I remember walking along, talking to God, and coming back up to the house. As

I was coming up the hill something flashed in my mind, something that was a result of the space I was in from the trip. What flashed in my mind was a phrase.

I know that when lots of times you take an ibogaine trip you get something that's enigmatic, you don't know what it is, and later on you'll get something that fills it in. Completes the sentence is really what it does. It turns out that "You're going to die," was part of a sentence. The second part of the sentence flashed into my mind. "Unless you stop taking codeine."

I rolled that one around and rolled it around and rolled it around and looked at it. God damn! How can I function, unless I take codeine? I just played around with it a lot. Maybe I haven't got the right message, or something like that. Then I said, "No, Jacob, don't fuck around with this stuff. You know the answer. You take it. You got the right message. Take it, just as you got it. I'm going to die unless I stop taking codeine. Okay, I got the message. That's the truth, I know that's the truth. So, what am I going to do about it? Am I going to quit taking codeine? It doesn't bother me to die. I'm going to die some day. But... I'm not ready yet. I don't want to, right now. Am I going to quit taking codeine?"

And it flashed in my mind the answer, this statement. "Jacob, that's the wrong question. The question is not 'Are you going to quit taking codeine?' The question is, 'Have you quit taking codeine?'" The same thing that happened with the cigarettes.

And I knew the answer. Right then and there I knew the answer. I had quit. I had quit. For a long, long time. My migraines got less and less. Occasionally they would get real strong, I would take some for a little while. But it was over with. I was over taking it as I used to. Well as you can imagine, that was a very spectacular thing in my life.

Those are personal incidents. Some of the rough times that I went through. Then I got some other people interested. In fact, some of the people I used to work with—I was doing groups then, tool was telling people about my experience and they all got excited and interested and said, "Hey! I'd like to do that!"

Fine! Somebody had said to me at one point, "Jacob, you should be doing this. You'd be a natural at this kind of thing."

I said, "Who me? I can't do that kind of thing. That'd be too big a responsibility. I wouldn't know how to handle it."

But this person whom I knew very well wanted to have a trip and I made the arrangements and I gave her a trip and she had a fabulous experience. And that was the beginning. Several people wanted to have a trip. But after a dozen or so had had a trip they were complaining because there was nobody they could talk to about it. Look, you couldn't talk to anybody about it. They wouldn't understand it, they'd think it was a terrible thing or something. So I said, "Fine, let's have a meeting at my house. Everybody who's tripped, we all get together and talk about our trip." We did that several times. They'd talk about it, we enjoyed it very much and one day somebody said, "Jacob, why don't we all take a trip together?" Somebody suggested I should be doing group trips, too.

I said, "What?" They were all clamoring about it. So I said, "Okay, we can try it once. We can all spend a weekend together and we'll have a trip."

There were ten or twelve of us. We had a little ceremony developed and plenty of preparation and security, and I stayed straight. I only let them take 50 micrograms of LSD because I didn't know what the hell was going to come from it. Well, a few of them turned on a little bit. Not very many of them did turn on. But I wasn't going to go any further that time. After it was over we talked about it and had a good time for the weekend, but not much happened.

I decided we'll do it again, only next time I will give them their base amount which I knew from their individual trip. They'd all had individual trips with me. Then we'll see what happens. We did that again about a month later and that was a fantastic experience. That began the whole program of group tripping.

There's the individual trip and the group trip. The evolvement is something I would like to be able to describe. There was so much that went on. It was all experimental, all exploring, everything that we did. We tried this, we tried that, in terms of what went on during a trip. First, I want to go into the development of the individual trip.

In the early days, whenever I had an individual trip, I always had a physician present. He would come in and see the person first and check them out. It was just a procedure that I wanted to explore and see what was necessary and what wasn't. This was mostly for my own feeling of security in case anything happened. He was present the first couple of hours of every trip. These trips were all done in my office. I had a folding bed that I put up and went through a lot of preparation with them first. I explored different things. I read everything there was about what was important to do in preparation for a trip. I tried a lot of them.

A physician worked with me a lot. He liked to work with people throughout the whole trip. I started to do that and then very gradually did less and less of it, until finally I did not work with them except at a point when they wanted me or needed me. He explored on a psychoanalytic basis. He used that model which I couldn't use. It was not my model.

It was less than a year that my doctor friend would come into the office. After that I didn't need anybody. I knew I didn't need anybody. In fact, it was better not to have him. He would try to do some work with the person which was anti what I was doing.

In the beginning I worked with the people on trips—I can't describe what the work was right now. I helped support them in turning on. They got frightened, you know? I'd hold their hands or I'd hold them in my arms and tell them to go ahead, experience it out. I would talk to them in advance about this so that they would know that this was available.

Most of them were blissful trips, but if somebody got frightened with the transition point between one stage of consciousness and the other I would prefer to be close to them. At times I would ask what they were experiencing. If they were in pain or something like that I would ask them to describe the pain, where it was, and go into it. If it was a pain in the stomach, I would say, "Okay, now, think about opening your mouth, and going down into your mouth and describe what you see. It's dark, it's this, that, and keep on going. Describe what you see as you go down. Go all the way down, into your insides." Frequently they would burst into a beautiful world of paradise. The pain would immediately be transformed into ecstasy. Something like that would happen. I tried many different things. As they were coming down from the trip we would talk, and they would talk about where they'd been. You can't talk much, you know, until you're coming down.

Also there was physical contact. It was important in those days that they would have something to resist before they turned on. Or as they were turning on. They were having trouble turning on—I'd tell them first that this might happen—I would lie down on top of them, grab the edge of the bed and say, "Now what I want you to do is push against me." I want you to know, I hung on for dear life. I said, "Push harder, harder, harder!" And they did. When they succeeded in getting me off they were through to the other side! Their report of what happened as a result of that and later what they experienced was just a fascinating thing.

One of the things I had everybody do that I tripped was after or as soon as he or she could sit down and make notes of whatever he or she could recall, and write up the whole thing—for themselves, and for me.

Myron: Did you keep copies of these reports?

Jacob: I kept a file of these reports, but some years ago, the file got thrown out. Of all the trips—I had hundreds of them—they would have made a good book themselves.

The screening process and the preparation process: we talked a lot. I had them go through a lot of rituals for themselves—fasting, learn how to do some fasting. I had certain things that I had them read, spiritual literature that was very illuminating and they were able to get it.

Myron: Do you have a few favorites along those lines?

Jacob: Not any more. Not any more, I don't. I don't suggest readings any more, because the people that come to me have gone through a lot of things in terms of reading, and they're ready for something besides reading.

Myron: I'm thinking in terms of people who are just looking into this, and looking for some helpful ways to get started.

Jacob: Very little that I've come across I would recommend. Aldous Huxley's Doors of Perception and Heaven and Hell, those certainly are ones. Those are the only things I found that were important. I used to give a lot of reading, but that didn't make any difference. This experience is such a very different dimension. They left it all behind very quickly. It did not help in getting them prepared. Their greatest help was their contact with me—talking and experiencing. For the most part the people that I do now are people who make a big difference in the world, with people. They're therapists and psychiatrists, physicians, they're government people who have very high positions and great influence.

Myron: I've always had this dream that you could somehow bring this about, yet we have never succeeded at that at our Foundation (the International Foundation for Advanced Study in Menlo Park, California).

Jacob: They didn't give you the chance.

Myron: I don't know; we brought a lot of stuff on ourselves. We were pretty immature.

Jacob: Of course. I look at the progress I made down through the years and the different changes that I made as a result of my experience—I can't recall them all but I continually changed my procedures and my thinking about it and my ideas about what happened and what could happen; how to set situations so that you get the best possible setting and so that they could get the best possible trip. The most useful trip for them.

Some of the rough things that I went through on trips, the roughest of all is they get paranoid and run away. That's scary as hell until they are located. They see me as the devil. No matter what I say to them the devil is trying to destroy them. If I try to get them to take some niacin, which is supposed to bring them down, that's poison. They won't touch it. No way. Or a sedative or whatever. I learned not to do that; I learned to screen better. I could sense after a while whether a person was likely to get paranoid on a trip, or violent, or something like that. And I was alone on all this.

This was such a fascinating thing to be doing! I didn't have to do much of anything at all except provide the opportunity and the material and then to see the fantastic results! The transformations that came in all of those people. It was really something.

We went on, I kept on doing it, one or two a month.

CHAPTER II

SELECTION AND PREPARATION: SELECTING THE CLIENT

MYRON: WHAT WOULD YOU look for when you screened? What were the characteristics that were important to avoid?

Jacob: I screened very carefully. I'll try to tell you what my screening process was. A lot of it was based upon experience. Not knowing at first who was a suitable candidate for the kind of trip I did under the circumstances I set up, I would offer to trip people who weren't suitable. As a result I had some pretty paranoid trips. That's *extremely* painful to go through, to stay with them until they finally come down. Even though afterwards they said it was the most fantastic experience they ever had in their life. It changed their whole life. That always happened when they had those paranoid trips. Painful experiences, weeping, listless; I was very encouraged when they could go through this.

One of the things I learned about tripping very early was that we get in touch with feelings we've never been able to experience before and at a depth and a level that we've never been able to reach. That could be fear, it could be love, it could be ecstasy, it could be *anything.* Just as long as it's feelings—sadness, grief. Lots of times they would start to cry on a trip and cry for the *longest* time so deeply. To me it seemed so satisfying because they were getting *something out.* I liked that.

I learned to watch out for my motivations for wanting to trip somebody. To make sure that—I don't know what word would be suitable here—I use the word pure, but it's not the word I want. Clean. That I wasn't doing it for self-aggrandizement or something like that. I learned very early that I am an instrument. I do not bring this experience to anybody. I provide them with the opportunity; *they* have the experience. They bring their own experience to themselves, and I have the privilege of sitting with them while it's going on.

Myron: I think I've picked up an awful lot of junk sitting in sessions. I was so inexperienced and I'd never been trained as a therapist and I used to get *so tired*. I'm sure it was my self involvement I wanted to do something for somebody.

Jacob: To try to help them. I very soon learned that my traditional techniques of helping people in therapy do not work, they just don't work. *Just leave 'em alone!* They know what the hell's wrong with them or the God within them knows what's wrong with them and provides them with whatever they need which I don't know anything about and *they* don't even know anything about. They don't know what their real needs are. All they know is what their wants are. That's true for all of us, of course. (Laughs.)

Just how you know you have a good candidate is very difficult to describe. I've tried to relate this many times. I've tried to teach. It's nothing you can teach. Only your experience will give it to you. My intuition was the most important thing, and my stomach. My stomach would respond to something that was not right. Something they would say—or just being with them, no matter what they were saying, because I couldn't trust what they were saying as being them. It isn't them, what they were saying. I would get a vague feeling of anxiety that would stay with me after I had talked to the person and certain questions, certain things that they had said would come to my mind.

I would just look at them. Then I would talk to them again a time or two and see if I wanted to proceed more along the exploring. Always I told them this is exploratory until I was really sure I wanted to trip with them and they were really sure that they wanted to take the trip. Then we would arrange for the trip and do some preparation.

Myron: Would you describe it as you would have to feel a certain kind of bond with them?

Jacob: Yes. I would have to have that feeling that I would really like to trip this person.

Other factors besides those subjective ones: How much work they have done on themselves in terms of their own individual growth. How long they've been working on themselves. What training they've had. What workshops they've gone to. What readings they've done. What they feel they've accomplished. How far they've gone and what their complaints were about themselves in terms of inadequacies, like, "I know all the things in my mind, but I want to get them in my heart." I can tell in getting their history if they're searching, how far they've gone, how much of it has sunk in. When I get the feeling that I'm really interested in this person, like, "Oh, boy, a trip would do just exactly what they want, what they're asking for!" Then I knew this was o.k. If I didn't get that kind of thing I wouldn't stay with them longer or I would say no, I don't think it's time yet.

I had to turn down people very seldom because before they even get to me there's always a selective process going on. They are referred by somebody who knows me and has tripped with me and has worked with me. Before they even get to know who I am or get to see me this person will call me and tell me, "You know, here's so-and-so that I would like to refer to you for a trip."

I would say, "Well, tell me about the person." They would tell me a lot of things—how well you know them, do you trust the person, a lot of questions. Questions are what you want. "What do you know about the explorations that they've made already? You know that we are spiritually oriented. Are they also interested in that and oriented in that?" They know these are questions I'm going to be asking, so that the people that are referred to me are already screened by them as good candidates. It might be the spouse of somebody that has tripped, too. A boyfriend or a girlfriend of somebody or a colleague or somebody who is on the search with them.

In other words they know this person. They've already screened them. The person really wants to have a trip. They know that. They just don't know where to go or how to go and they've heard what great things have come from them, and what great things have happened to the person that is making the referral. They're close, in some way. They'd like to have that happen to them, too.

Then the referring person calls me, because no one can ever give out my name without prior clearance from me. They call me, I get all the information. I say, "Yep, it sounds okay. Tell them to call me and I'll set up an exploratory with them."

And that's what happens. Very rarely do I have to turn anybody like that down. Very rare. Although sometimes I don't have the right feeling about the person and I know that the person who referred them doesn't know much about them, really, but just believes they might be a good candidate. That one I would turn down.

There are these particular questions, some of them I've mentioned that I think of now that I would ask them or explore with them in terms of their state. What their expectations are. What they'd like to get from such an experience. I used to see them six, eight, ten times before I would decide. Not anymore. One visit is all I need. One visit with the person for me to experience them and to get the feeling, "Yeah, this is one I really would like to trip." Or for them to get to experience me, for that's very important to them. The feeling of trust that they have in me is extremely important. How do they feel about me? When it turns out that we really make a connection, that's all there is to it, we arrange a trip. No more than that. All the circumstance surrounding the trip, that I'll be talking about some place along the line, too.

So, it's mostly based upon the experience that I've had already and it's mostly a feeling and an intuitive process which I don't see operating, I just see the results which come in my willingness to relate to a person.

Myron: Are there certain kinds of presenting problems which are a factor, like certain kinds of difficulties that a person has that make it a more difficult situation or is it more just a feel of the individual?

Jacob: You see, the point of presenting symptoms, specific problems that they want to have dealt with, doesn't come into the picture. There are no symptoms, really. They just say, "I would like to have this kind of experience because I want to grow, as so-and-so has been doing. I want to get the kind of religious experience that can come out of this thing. That's what I'm looking for."

They will come in, and I'll ask, "What do you want to take a trip for?" Then they'll tell me what's going on in their life that they're dissatisfied with, that they'd like to come to terms with, that they'd like to change. They have lots of anxieties, worried about things—they're not getting along well with their job, with their boss, with their wife, with their family, colleagues or friends or whatever or they've got complaints, presenting complaints. It's not the kind of thing that you find when somebody comes in for therapy and they give you a list of their neurotic symptoms or something like that and that they want to have changed. Sure they want change. Many of them have already gone far enough to learn that it's not the outside that needs changing, it's the inside that needs changing and this is the approach that they want to take for changing the inside. Because when you change the inside what you see outside is different.

Myron: So the people you work with would generally be far more growth-oriented than what the usual therapist works with.

Jacob: Mostly, yes. Every now and then somebody comes from some part of the country that is a person who is referred by somebody whom I've trained out there who does a lot of tripping, too.

Myron: Would it appeal to you if somebody had some unusually tough problem that they were unable to get anywhere with in therapy and they thought that maybe this procedure might be a breakthrough and might be helpful? Would that kind of a case interest you?

Jacob: That's a familiar thing. They say, "I've been working on this for a *long time* and I haven't been able to get any place with it. Maybe a trip will help me break through it." I've heard this. It could be a specific thing or it could be a general condition that they talk about.

Myron: Most people have a resistance to therapy. They don't like the idea that something's wrong with them and that they've got to go for help. In another case it might be the expense, or whatever, so usually before a lot of people will go into therapy there has to be some really tough problem. Maybe they've got colitis, or maybe they have a serious marriage problem or they know they have a very difficult relationship and maybe they've worked in therapy for a long period of time and haven't seemed to get anywhere. They seem to be really blocked.

Jacob: I see what you're saying. A number of people like that were referred to me and referred by people who know them and know their history. And I say, "Look, I can tell you about something that very possibly may help you break through on this."

Myron: To focus on this issue, maybe they're not even interested in spiritual growth but they just really have a serious problem.

Jacob: Oh, yes, that's right! I never mention the word spiritual to them unless *they* bring it up. I've had *many* people, I mean *many* people who've come to me who have been in analysis for a long time. Some have been in analysis four times a week for eight to ten years continuously. They said they had gotten a lot out of it. However, there was always something that they never could get to. They have taken a trip and in *one* trip afterwards have said, "I got more out of that one day's experience than I did in my whole eight or ten years or whatever of psychoanalysis." I've done that *numbers* of times.

Clients with Previous Psychedelic Experience

Here's another one that happens a lot. People will come to me who have already tripped who want to have my particular kind of way of tripping. One of them had tripped at least five hundred times on acid, others who have tripped three, four hundred times, down through the early Sixties, clear up to recent times. You know, *plenty* of trips their own way, who've heard about people who have tripped with me and where they got to so they want to have this kind of trip. We talk about it, and they would be good candidates so I'd say, "Sure." They would have their trip on acid. *Invariably* these people have said, "I've never had an acid trip before in my life! This is the first time I've ever really had an acid trip."

Myron: I'm real interested in that, because frankly I've had a lot of resistance to Tim Leary and the tremendous effort he made to make it so generally available. I feel that so much of the potential has been missed by kids using it on their own in the way they've used it. There's been a lot of self-gratification, there's been a lot of pleasure experiences and a lot of what Al Hubbard called "sharpening your wits" to reinforce "I'm right, you're wrong." I feel by and large that not too many have seen the real implications. So your experience here really interests me.

Jacob: Yeah. I would always ask them, "Did you feel that you ever got any value from your previous trips?"

They would say, "I got some great insights from it." They would say that in advance. But afterwards they would say, "No, *nothing* like what I got this time."

Myron: I think that's really marvelous. It says a great deal for you and your procedures. And it confirms some of my own hopes in this area. Did you keep any kind of records where you might be able to give some kind of a numerical assessment for this sort of thing? Like, how many individuals came to you who had many, many acid trips who arrived at this conclusion as a result of a single trip?

Jacob: I didn't keep any records but I can give you a fair estimate. Looking over more than 3,000 people who have tripped with me individually and in groups I would say that between five and ten percent have tripped before. That's on psychedelics, not just grass. Certainly five percent have tripped; some a little bit, some a lot. It's those who have tripped a lot—well they will *all* say that the trip they do with me is very different, very different.

Myron: You can say that that's just about universal?

Jacob: Yes. For those who have tripped before on acid or any of the psychedelics or psychoactive materials even, except for grass. Yeah. Once or twice a number of them—I can't recall now how many—have had very bad trips and came to me to have a trip under *these* circumstances. Usually where they were interrupted, and unable to get all the way through it because somebody took them off to the hospital and they were given Thorazine or some kind of shit like that. They didn't get a chance to really complete it, to go through all the bad spaces that they had to go through. They would come to me and we would trip. Under my circumstances I helped them through their fears so that when they came out they were really reborn. That's Stan Grof's whole model, that's a rebirth experience. Transformation is rebirth and all that.

Clients in Therapy

Myron: Do you think you can make an estimate of how many had been in extensive therapy who as a result of a trip with you found that they had made a really profound gain compared to the therapy they had previously been in?

Jacob: Yeah. How many had been in therapy—a *lot* of them. Let me see if I can say how many. Eighty to eighty-five percent had been in therapy before. Some of them were currently in therapy and wanted to have this experience. I want to come back to that, so you remind me of that. Out of that eighty to eighty-five percent, whatever it is, all of them said they got much more out of their tripping.

Now, they're not putting down their therapy. In fact, this experience illuminated the insights that they got from therapy but didn't get very deeply. It validated their therapy. For many people, too—I don't know how many, it would be hard to estimate this—it brought them to the realization that they wasted all of their God damned time; they didn't get a thing out of therapy. They worked hard at it, stayed long at it, many of them, labored at it, and thought there was something wrong with them. In fact, they had just gotten with the wrong person, that's all. If anybody came to me that was in therapy I first stipulated I cannot bring you this experience unless you get clearance from your therapist. There was an immediate screening process taking place. There were those who said they couldn't do that, they just didn't want to tell him about it.

I said, "That's quite a commentary on the relationship you have with your therapist. I can't do this. I will not do it. If you tell your therapist that you want to do this I need assurance that he agrees that it's okay for you to do it. I'd like for him to talk to me if he wants to." No, I stopped doing that. I didn't want to be identified.

Myron: I was going to ask you about the exposure.

Jacob: I want the therapist to know that the person I'm talking to about this has already agreed not to reveal my identity to anybody without prior clearance from me. That's the *first requirement* I give to anybody.

Myron: So if they went back to their therapist to get clearance they would say, "I've found somebody that's real good to take a trip with," and the therapist asks, "Who is it?" They'd have to say, "I can't tell you."

Jacob: Right away that would bust up the relationship.

Myron: I can see where a lot of therapists would really get on their high horse about that. On the other hand, were there any who got to know you and would keep the trust and even be willing to refer their patients to you?

Jacob: Most of the therapists who would do that have tripped themselves. I always warned the person who was in therapy that, "I want you to understand and realize that it's quite possible that after you've had your trip you will terminate your therapy." Invariably it happened. In a very few cases they could keep on working with the therapist. They could do that if the therapist had tripped. But you cannot trip and work with a therapist who hasn't tripped and get any value out of it. You can't relate back and forth. You can't trip as a patient and work with a therapist who has not tripped because he has not had the experience and you cannot relate to him about it. It ends up that I can only trip people who are in therapy with a therapist who understands tripping and is willing to refer.

Let me mention something about my original position when I first started out. I had the traditional psychological or psychiatric attitude towards this stuff. This is dangerous, this is bad, you shouldn't do it, and anybody who does it is crazy, and all that kind of stuff. That was my position in that regard.

There's no easy way to satori. You've got to work hard and you've got to suffer. I was like the typical Christian who didn't have much confidence in grace. Yet I knew what grace was. I did experience grace many times. I had to overcome all of those prejudices first before I could really explore honestly and openly. And of course my first trip dispelled *all* my doubts. My own first trip. Since then there was never any problem.

Myron: Would you care to say approximately how many therapists you have provided the experience for?

Jacob: In all categories—psychiatrists, M.D.s, psychologists, psychiatric social workers, transactional analysis people, all the different schools that exist where people see patients whether they're licensed or unlicensed, there's quite a spread of all of them—altogether, a hundred and fifty. That's what comes to my mind. It's over a period of fifteen years since I've been really doing it.

Myron: And these are all people who would have a practice of their own where they would be counseling others.

Jacob: Right. People-helpers—that includes nurses, physical therapists, people who are very important to other people. At times I would get referrals from them.

Myron: Of the roughly 150 people-helpers you have worked with, how many are actually psychiatrists and psychologists?

Jacob: I would say about one-fourth. The others are psychiatric social workers, family counselors, professional helpers like that.

Myron: Well gosh, you've started a real significant movement here.

Jacob: (Laughs.) It extends very much around the world, really.

Myron: It's been kept very, very quiet, it seems to me.

Jacob: The selective process has helped with that. The security practices that everybody's imbued with right from the beginning. That's what's important. I've been able to function this way. Yes, it's underground, and all of that. I've been able to function this way for all of these years because I trust the people and they know about our security situation. A few people have broken security. It has happened. Nothing has come from it, of course. They've told somebody who tripped them.

Security Problems

Myron: Security must have been a terrible problem. Can you say more about what it's like to work under such conditions?

Jacob: We were always security-conscious and we made everybody who came in contact with us security-conscious. Most people were able to really be ethically security-conscious and a few weren't. The few who weren't who talked about it, maybe blabbed, talked unnecessarily or identified people—no harm has ever come from that.

You see, again, a spiritual trip is what's involved here. This I have to say—it's the only way I know how to talk about it what I do and even how I do it is not up to me. I'm guided. I can't define that, I can't explain it. I know that that's true. If I wasn't supposed to be doing this, and I've said this before, I wouldn't be doing it. If God didn't want me to do it He would have stopped me a *long time ago*. I have a lot of faith that that's true. At the same time I keep a close eye on my integrity and my security. Everybody else's security is bound up in mine. We're all in it together.

I definitely have suffered, I have suffered considerably with fears, what I call "just in case" fears or "what if" fears. What if we're sitting there, laying there and having a trip, you know, everybody's all laid out and stoned out of their God damned mind, their pupils are as big as saucers, and somebody knocks on the door and it's the police raiding us. I don't know *how many times* that's come across my mind. What if somebody died on a trip? What if—I don't know, all the "what ifs" that I had—what if somebody freaked out and ran down the street screaming? *That happened!!* Paranoia! Everybody has it, I know, and I have it! If I hadn't been doing *this* to be paranoid about, I'd be doing something else to be paranoid. It's only since I've taken the Course in Miracles that I've gotten over my guilt and my fears.

Many years and many times I'd be in much agony falling asleep, and wake up in the morning and have it hit me. That's true. I've looked at it and I've said, "Jacob, for Christ's sake what are you exposing yourself to all this shit for? You don't need it." Then I'd look and I'd say, "Look at the people. Look what's happening to them." I'd say, "Is it worth it? Is it worth going through all of this shit for that?" Inevitably I'd come back with "Yeah, it's worth it." Especially at the end of a weekend when I'd see what fantastic things have happened to these people. I would say *clearly* to myself, "Jacob, it is *worth* it! Whatever you have to go through. It's *worth* it to produce these results!"

Security has been a terrible problem. It hasn't been a problem in that sense, but like I'm describing now. What I've gone through because of fear of discovery. This is a part of security. Actually, my worst fears in every situation have been realized. I have said many, many times, whatever you are afraid of never happens. And I know that's true. And yet sometimes the exact incident that you're afraid of happening does happen. However, what you were afraid would be the consequences did not happen. So what you're afraid of didn't happen. That's happened in my life a number of times. Some of them have been in connection with psychedelics, with what I'm doing. There are those people who know that I'm doing some thing. I believe they know the kind of work I'm doing and know that it's under very good control and a creative process. They don't bother me. They won't do anything to me. You'd be surprised at the different walks of life people have come from for tripping.

Preparation

I'll bring my analogies in here at this point. When I'm talking about a trip to a person who hasn't tripped and they want to know, "What's it like?" It's hard to describe what it's like but I have a couple of analogies that I use.

One is, imagine that you're on a stage, a very large stage, a round stage, circular. You're standing in the center of the stage. Around this stage is a huge curtain, very, very high and it's closed and where the curtain comes together there's about say three feet of space, of an opening. You're standing in the middle of that stage and you're looking out through that opening. Everything you see is the totality of your experience of yourself. What happens on a trip is by some mysterious means the curtain very gradually is pulled back. Very gradually. It's pulled back until it's pulled all the way around the back and you're given the opportunity to see everything that's been there all the time but you couldn't see it before because there was a curtain. *All* the different levels of experience that it's possible to have, you have. All the different truths, all the different things, you have. You experience it. Then, as you start to come down, very gradually the curtain gets pulled back around until you're all the way down.

When you're all the way down, the difference is that before, you had about three feet of space that was open to look through. You now have about fifteen feet of space. You have really expanded your awareness, which is what they call these materials, awareness-expanders.

Myron: The curtain might have even gotten a little transparent.

Jacob: Yeah, (laughs), that was what I was going to follow with. In addition to that you have a lot of memory of what you did experience before. So in a sense that's true, the curtain has become almost transparent. You don't remember everything, you don't need to remember everything. You don't need to. You remember everything you need to remember.

There's another analogy that I use, too. It's similar to that. That is, imagine a castle, a huge castle, very large. Many rooms, many turrets, many levels of it. There's only one way to get into this castle, and that's the front door. The front door is *solid steel. Impregnable.* You can knock on that door all you want. You can do everything you can to tear it down. You can 't get it down. Every now and then you might somehow or other move it a little bit to get a glimpse of what's behind it, but that's all. There's no way, and you've tried every way possible to get into that castle—which is yourself.

What happens on a trip is by some mysterious magic means this door is dissolved, and you have the opportunity to go in and explore that castle. Any place you want. You go in and you look around, and you find many wonderful places, strange places maybe, scary places and all that. You can go to the top and you can go to the bottom and you get a sense of what the totality of yourself really is like. As you come down, what happens is that the door somehow or other gets back up there. But that's all right, because you have a memory of what possibilities are there and what you've experienced. The biggest experience that it brings to you is that it connects you with feelings that you've never been connected with before. They are now open to you. Not on the level or the intensity that you had in the experience but certainly much more than they ever were before. That gives them an idea. "My God!" they say. "How soon can I have one?" (Laughter.)

Myron: God, Jacob, those are so good. I think of places where I can use those analogies myself. Do you have any objection if I use them?

Jacob: It's the greatest privilege in the world for me to be able to share them, so if they're of value to other people they're welcome to them.

Myron: One of the problems that you run into is that very often you get people who have rather powerful internal conflicts and it's really difficult for them to confront them and they'll dodge and go off in different directions. Did you ever do anything to try to encourage them to confront that sort of thing? Similar to the way you described if it manifested as a pain—you had a beautiful technique for dealing with that. Did you have some other techniques along those lines?

Jacob: Yes, yes. Whenever I was aware of anything like that—whenever they'd get really frightened—I'd ask them to, "Look at what you're afraid of, just look at what you're afraid of. All you have to do is just look at it; don't do anything about it, just look at it. Just keep on looking at it and just tell me what you experience when you're looking at it." Most of the times they'll go off into some kind of a visual trip. Experience something. But they were not experiencing a specific block that you do experience consciously. It wasn't that. It was a painful fear. That's what I had them live with and stay with until it became transformed. As it did, the block was gone. I don't think we even knew what the block was. It was not a specific fear. It seemed to me at the time that it was an *accumulation* of all the unfaced fears that was being expressed at that time. By facing them they dissolved them-to some degree at least.

Myron: One of the marvelous things about this is the honesty—that once you're willing to face it, it becomes resolved. This is one of the major uses of these substances, I think.

Jacob: I use an analogy with them when we're going through preparation. You know, if you're walking along and there's someone behind you and you're worried or scared about it and you start to run, the more you run in fear from it the greater the monster becomes. Once you stop and turn around it turns out to be some little silly funny thing, and their fear disappears. There're many little anecdotes like that that I would give in preparation for trips.

Photographs

One of the things I have them do for the trip is to get a bunch of pictures from a list that I give them. These pictures actually as you'll see are a history of their lives. They go back home or get them wherever they are or write for them. They get all the pictures that they can and bring them to wherever they are. Then I ask them to select the pictures in a particular manner which is really very important. I say, "Give yourself *plenty of time.* First let me give you the list of pictures that I want you to get." Here's the list:

1. Starting with the pictures of themselves, one at age two and one every two years thereafter through adolescence, sixteen or eighteen.

2. A picture of their mother and a picture of their father when they were young but they can still remember their mother and their father, and a recent picture of each.

3. Same thing about each of their siblings, an early one that they remember that way and a recent one of their siblings and their families if they have one.

4. A picture of a grandparent that was significant in their life.

5. A picture of any aunts, uncles, or cousins that were significant in their life.

6. If they're married, I ask them to bring some wedding pictures because wedding pictures usually have all the relatives and it gives them a chance to see them. If they don't have any pictures I'll say a picture of the woman you married either just before you married her or when you got married, an early picture. And a recent one of her or him, as the case may be.

7. If there are children, a picture of the children when they were about two years old which is when they begin to start to have a little personality of their own. And a recent one of each. And if they are married, with their families. And even if they're not married, a picture of any woman or man who has had great significance in their life. Lovers, current or past or whatever.

8. I ask them to select the pictures in this manner: Gather them all together-boxes, albums, however they are, and put them in front of you, and start with one. The top one or anything like that. Pick it up and look at it. Just look at it to see what you experience in connection with that picture. Look at it a little while. You may not experience anything. It's all right. Put it aside, pick up the next one, then look at it. If it provokes any memories, kind a sit with the memories a little bit, let them go where they want to go. Whatever feelings you have, allow them to be there. Whenever you come across a picture that's on the list, set it aside in a separate pile. Go through *all* the pictures you've got, every single one of them, doing that. You may have to have two or three sittings to do it. I ask them to do it no further away than a week before the trip, as close to the time of the trip as they can. I want to tell you something. That really turns them on. When they come they're in the middle of their trip.

CHAPTER III

THE INDIVIDUAL TRIP

MYRON: LET'S GET INTO your procedures.

Jacob: All right. I'll start with the individual trip first, because the group trip follows the individual one. The first trip is always with LSD. I like to start at eight o'clock in the morning. I like to do it preferably in their own home, if it's convenient, secure, and nobody's going to be there, nobody's going to interrupt, and it isn't too far away for me to go to. (Laughs.) I get there maybe a half hour before that, before eight.

I set up my equipment. My equipment consists of headphones, two face masks, a cassette player and separate recorder, tapes for music, and a special cup. (Jacob shows the box he takes along with him.) I carry these along with me which is part of my ritual that I have. I talk about the transformation experience and how the cup is always a very important symbol of the transformation experience.

I have this setup with the earphones coming out of this machine. This is the way I play my music to them. Music is all on cassettes. The records scratch and they don't work very well at all. Then I have another tape recorder in there which is used to record everything that's said. I record the whole trip. I have a remote control here that I use so that I only turn it on when something's being said.

These are some of the things that I go over with them. The structure is first. Structure is a very important thing, and what structure is, is a set of agreements that I ask them to make with me. These are the things that I ask them to agree to with me:

1. They will not leave the house where we're having the trip at any time during the trip without prior clearance from me.

2. They agree that there will be no physical harm or violence to themselves or to me or to anything else in the house.

3. Reiteration of the security requirement. They agree they will not reveal to anybody else where and with whom they had this trip without prior clearance from me, ever.

4. I ask them to agree—now if this is a woman or somebody gay—I ask them to agree that there will be no sex taking place between us. I'll explain the background for these agreements in a minute.

5. The last one I ask them to agree is that at any time during the trip if anything is going on and I tell them to stop it, stop doing it, and I make clear, "This is under structure; it's not just a recommendation or suggestion," they agree that they will stop it. Or if I tell them to do something and I make clear it's under structure they agree that they will do it. I tell them to look at this one very, very carefully, because when they agree to that they are virtually putting their lives in my hands and the only thing they have to go on is whatever faith they have in me—that I would never let them do anything that would be harmful to themselves, nor would I ever require anything of them that would be harmful to them. These are bills to faith. That puts them back on their faith, see.

I review it, and then I say, "Do you have any questions or qualifications or anything that you want to know about it?" When they say no, I say, "Do you agree to abide by this structure?" They say, "Yes." I say, "Thank you."

Now, the first one, not to leave the house: I don't want them wandering around without prior agreement. Sometimes when they're coming down from a trip if they want to go out and walk around because it is so beautiful, fine, I'll walk with them. They ask and they check with me.

Physical harm and violence: Sometimes people are afraid they're going to be angry, they're always talking about the unexpressed anger that they've got. They're afraid that might happen so when they make that agreement they feel safe about the anger, they're not going to destroy anything or hurt anybody.

The fourth one about sex: Sometimes women get real turned on. Sexually they get really connected with their sexuality and they're scared, they don't know what to do with it so they'll tend to squelch it. I don't want them to do that. I want them to find it and hang on to it and know that they're safe, nothing's going to happen. The same thing with a gay person. If it comes up, let it come up, what the hell.

Okay. They've agreed to abide by this structure. I ask them to read this, a late 17th century prayer. It's the only thing I've ever found down through the years that *really* is the most suitable for beginning a trip. I ask them to read it quietly to themselves once and read it through a second time:

> *Lord, I know not what I ought to ask of thee;*
> *Thou only knowest what I need;*
> *Thou lovest me better than I know how to love myself.*
> *O Father, give to Thy child that which*
> *he himself knows not how to ask.*
> *I dare not ask either for crosses or for consolations;*
> *I simply present myself before thee,*
> *I open my heart to Thee.*
> *Behold my needs which I know not myself;*
> *see and do according to Thy tender mercy.*
> *Smite, or heal; depress me or raise me up;*
> *I adore all Thy purposes without knowing them;*
> *I am silent; I offer myself in sacrifice;*
> *I yield myself to Thee: I would have no*
> *other desire than to accomplish Thy will.*
> *Teach me to pray.*
> *Pray Thyself in me.*
> *AMEN.*
>
> – *François de Salignac Fenelon*
> *Archbishop of Cambray, 1651–1715, AD*

Then we have a dropping ceremony, and I explain the cup and I have water in it and I have the capsule with their medicine in it, too. After they've read the prayer then I give it to them. I've already explained the significance of the cup as a symbol of transformation all the way back to Jesus and to earlier days and all that kind a stuff. I have them take the cup and the capsule, swallow the medicine whatever it happens to be, and drink the water from the cup.

After this dropping ceremony I ask to see their pictures. I have them organize them according to this list, their own pictures first with the youngest on top and the oldest one on the bottom. Their youngest age and the oldest. Same with the mother and father and all the relatives if there's any chronological period of time that's involved. The last one I ask them to look at is their wife or lover currently.

Just before that I organize them all in this fashion: First the pictures of themselves, then the mother, then the father. Now, some of the other pictures will have mother and father in them, too. They may have some very significant picture show up that isn't on that list for mother, father, family, or something like that. A house that they lived in or a pet that they had, goodness knows what, maybe an army picture. Whatever really gives them an emotional charge, positive or negative. That's what I call other significant pictures. They're to pull those out to really get to cover the ground there. Sometimes they bring too many, I screen them out.

Now, once they've dropped the medicine, I say, "Let's look at your pictures." They'll show them to me, and I arrange them in the order that I want to use them, and that's it. We don't take them apart and look at them. I set the organization and have them identified into their stacks, because we'll be doing that later. Then we sit and we talk. I ask them if they've had any dreams the night before or whatever. When they have them I say, "Well tell me about it." I just want them to tell me the dream. I frequently get something out of the dream.

I explain to them—and I've already talked about this before to them—but I say, "You know when you go along through the transition from one stage of consciousness to another one sometimes you run into difficulties. If you do, like if you get frightened or something like that, all you have to do is put out your hand. I'll see it, I'll be sitting right there. If not just say, 'Jacob.'" Their hand's out there, and I'll go over and I'll take their hand and put it in mine. No talking, or anything like that. I just hold it nice and firm and solid. God, what they say afterwards about what happened during that holding the hand, what a tremendous experience they had. If they want me to I'll put my arms around them and hold them in my arms. I encourage them when they get frightened to stay with it, don't try to do anything about it, just let yourself be afraid. I explain to them I will be here all the time. I always have a security bucket and a package of kleenex, in case they get nauseated they've got the bucket there.

We'll sit and talk about different things until they feel themselves starting to turn on. Then, fine, I ask them to go to the bathroom and empty their bladder, then come back and lie down. Then I put their eyeshades on, the earphones on, and cover them nice and cozy and comfortable and turn on the music. I tell them that I'll check in with them after an hour to see if they're turned on. They turn on with the music. Beautiful turn-on music, too.

Myron: How do you tell if they're turned on?

Jacob: What I do is I've got a microphone, see, and I'll turn on the microphone and I'll talk. I'll say, "(whatever their name is), do you feel turned on yet?"

They'll say, "Oh, yes."

I'll say, "Good. Have a good trip." And I just turn off the thing and let it go.

Or they'll stop and they'll think and say, "I'm not sure." I say, "Are you as turned on as you'd like to be?"

Sometimes they say, "No, I think I could be more turned on." I say, "Good, I'll give you a booster."

Or they'll say, "Gee, I'm really not sure. I haven't done this before. I don't know what it is to be fully turned on."

I say, "Okay. I'll check back with you again in fifteen minutes." I don't think they are, but I want to check back anyway, because sometimes they might turn on, it takes an extra fifteen minutes. I check back with them in fifteen minutes and I say, "Are you turned on now?" They'll still be questioning. As long as they're able to question they aren't turned on enough, I'll say, "Well, I'll give you a booster."

I check with them again thirty minutes later. Most of the times they are already turned on. If not, I give them another booster. If they're not really turned on I'll keep going until I check in and they say, "Oh, yeah." Sometimes I watch them, I can tell from the way they are. I can tell they're really stoned. They're going through quite a trip.

Myron: How long do you wait for the second booster?

Jacob: Thirty minutes. Between boosters, thirty minutes between any boosters until they're really turned on. A booster would go 125 micrograms unless not a thing's happening, they feel pleasant and all that but not a thing's happening. Then I'll give them 250 micrograms. I mention to them, "Look, sometimes you get real turned on by a piece of music and it's a great experience and it ends and you're kind of disappointed. All you have to do is say, 'Play it again,' and I'll play it again for you. You go right back out again."

I tell them that music is the vehicle that takes you to all the different places you go on your trip. Music is the vehicle that takes you to all the different places.

Myron: Isn't silence the vehicle sometimes?

Jacob: Oh yeah. I say, "If you ever want to be quiet, have silence, let me know." Most of the time they want the music. Oh yes.

Sometimes I'll just not play anything for a while but in just a little bit they'll say, "The music's off." You've never heard music in your life, really, you'll see that you've never really heard music in your life until you've heard it on the trip. Which is true, everybody knows who's had that. I tell them, "Anytime I'm playing a piece of music that's not consonant with where you are, that's bothering you or you don't like it, just say, 'Change the music,' and I will." Once in a while that happens. Most of the time with the kind of music I have they dig it all the way through.

I can tell when they're starting to come down because until that time they are absolutely still. Every now and then I've got to get down on the floor to look to make sure they're still breathing! (Laughs.) I do that as a kind of a ritual. I don't do it because I'm scared any more. (More laughter.) When they start to come down, they start to move around, they may want to go to the bathroom. Sometimes in the middle of the trip they want to go to the bathroom. That's fine, I take them in the bathroom and stay with them unless they want me to go outside. I ask them before they come out to stop and look in the mirror, the bathroom mirror. Just take a good look. They do, you know, God they report things—whatever they saw and all that. *Later.* Not during this visit. I take them back, lie them down, put them back.

All right. When they have come down enough that they're able to talk but they're still hallucinating a little bit—that may be five, six hours into the trip, around that time, some may be a little bit earlier, some may be a little bit later, seven or eight hours—and they're functional, they can move around, I have them get up. I've told them this is what'll happen. I have them get up and they go sit down at a table some place and we do the picture trip.

What the picture trip is, I start out with pictures of themselves. I have them in front of me. I take the first one and I hand it to them and I tell them, "Just look at it, just look at it and see what you experience. Look at it as long as you want to. When you're through looking at it, hand it back. If you have anything to say, fine. Say it. If not, you don't have to say anything." One at a time I hand them the pictures. The pictures, they don't react much to the two- to four-year-old pictures. Some time around the age of six is a very significant picture for them. That's the point in life where we lose our naturalness and we start taking on the acts of the world and behaving the way people tell us to and start squelching our own naturalness. Frequently they get to that picture and they start to cry. And cry and cry and cry. "Gee, what an unhappy face!" Or they say, "I don't know."

I'm taping everything that's being said. They'll do a lot of talking and a lot of crying. And a lot of ruminating, and remembering. This talking is very important to them later on when they go back and listen to it. It reconnects them with their whole experience. I give them the tape. After we've gone through all the pictures we just sit around. If they want to listen to music some more, fine. Listen to music. Then maybe about four o'clock in the afternoon, say, I arrange to have the babysitter come by.

I don't like to leave them alone on the day of their trip. I want to have somebody stay and spend the evening until they go to sleep or spend the night. It's got to be somebody they know, love, and trust, as well as somebody who has tripped if it's at all possible. Because somebody who has tripped knows how to serve somebody who's just tripped without asking a whole bunch of stupid questions that they can't answer. Just takes care of them, and just listens to them talk if they have something to say. Or leaves them alone if they want to be alone. I tell them, "I will not leave until you say it's okay for me to leave." The person who comes as their sitter may be their wife or husband. They may not have tripped but they may be the most suitable person. I brief that person about how to take care of things.

Myron: Generally in a marriage you have the partner absent during the trip?

Jacob: Only me and the person on the trip. Unless I'm doing a couples trip, but they've already tripped individually first. Although when the other one comes in there's quite a bit of relating that goes on because this person is so transformed and has come to a new level of feeling of love about their spouse or lover or whoever it may be. Then, oh, I might fix them a little plate of some fruit, crackers, or cheese or something to eat, you know some sensory thing, have a glass of wine, something like that. I stay with them and the sitter until it's okay for me to leave. I pack up my stuff and I go on home. And that's it.

I'm available for them to see or to call and I leave my number and everything. If anything comes up they want to call me about, anything at all, I tell them, "Don't hesitate at all, call me any time."

That's the individual trip.

CHAPTER IV

THE GROUP TRIP

JACOB: ONE OF THE THINGS that I've had a lot of experience with is the group trip. People get a great deal out of the group trip. It allows them to try a lot of different things, and connect with a lot of other individuals. The way we've worked it out, it lets them go through a progression of growth.

One of the most important things for a group trip is to have a nice setting. I have a very good friend in Washington, D.C., a psychiatrist who loves this work. He has a place on the western shore of the Chesapeake Bay, not too long a drive from the city. It's perfect—a nice view of the water, lots of trees, secluded, excellent security. We've been running group trips there for a long time. I used to fly out every month until his own people got so experienced it wasn't necessary any more.

We generally have between ten and twelve people come, trippers, and three gurus who stay straight. They all arrive Friday evening around eight o'clock and they greet each other with love and joy since they haven't seen each other since the last trip they had together. They meet the new people and the new people get to meet all of them. We only have one new person a weekend unless there's too many backed up. Then we'll take two new people a weekend. There'll be some snacks set out there for them to nibble on and they'll have some wine. It's a nice occasion until they all arrive. When they've all arrived and greeted each other, then we all gather in the living room and sit around the room.

The leader makes announcements about things and all of that. Then we induct the new people, the new person or people, into the structure of the group. It's the same set of agreements except no sex takes place during the weekend. This is a very important thing. I want to tell you how important this is. I'll tell you right now, otherwise I'll forget it.

The experience evokes such a tremendous feeling of love and closeness that people love to be close and hug each other and love each other. They have love puddles where they all get together and just hug each other and love each other. When they know there's not going to be any sex nobody's worried about what might happen. They can let go to their really loving feelings without being concerned about, "Is he trying to make out?" or, "Is she wanting me to make out?" or whatever. All these crazy thoughts that occur to people. Then they just have a *marvelous* time. That's after they've all come down, you know. But the instruction is that no sexual activity take place at any time during the weekend.

The last one is the same as the last one I gave about the individual trip—do what I tell you to do or stop doing what you're doing—it's the same structure. But now it's with the group. They're being inducted and everybody else is renewing the structure for themselves. The leader presents them with the questions and asks them if they agree and they say yes. He says, "Thank you," and they say, "Thank you," and then they go on.

The next thing is that the leader may read something or talk about something that he's currently working on or something like that. Not really much more. He asks, "When you talk tonight, I want you to just talk out of your experience and tell whatever's going on in your life that you want to share with us, whatever you're hoping will happen this weekend." There's a variety of things that he mentions.

By the way, the new person has already been briefed about the whole procedure for the whole weekend so they know what to expect. Then the leader says, "Who would like to start?" Somebody raises their hand and starts talking about where they're at, what's going on, what's happened since the last time. Anything that occurs to them. We ask them to talk to the whole group, not just talk to the leaders. We don't go around the circle, because no one should feel under pressure. Whatever they want to say, and as much as they want to say is fine.

It's only when you're ready to speak that you do it. There are frequent breaks. After about four persons there's a break. They all get up and pee, drink some water, have some more nibbles or something and talk and catch up on things until we've gone all the way through everybody. That includes the three staff. We all participate; we say what's going on in our lives, what we're into. And, as I've explained it to them, each comes there as a separate link, and in this process they forge the link into a chain, by this process of sharing with each other. You learn a lot, too. You sure do. And we see how far so-and-so has gone since the last time or whatever.

It takes a number of trips before you get to trip with everybody who comes, and you don't get to trip with everybody who comes because some people come once every six months or once a year so they're tripping with different people all of the time. There's always somebody there that they know from other trips, two or three maybe. So you really get the experience of a whole bunch of people.

Then the leader talks about going to bed—what happens is when they're ready to go to sleep, they stake out their pads where they're going to sleep. Pads with blankets. They pick places all around the house. When they're ready to go to sleep, they smoke some grass sometimes to help them to go to sleep. Whatever. It's all okay. When they want to go to sleep they go over to their pad, lie down, put the earphones on and there's music playing, going-to-sleep music, until they go to sleep. They wake up early in the morning, around 6:30, and complete their toilet. We ask them to be very quiet, not silent but quiet and reflective. If they meditate, do some meditating. Move around outside, just not a lot of unnecessary yacking. They follow that pretty well.

One at a time each person sits down at a table with me and the leader and we go over what medicine they're going to take. (The various agents available and their effects are described in Chapter 5.) We decide what they're going to take and how much. It depends upon what they're trying to achieve, what they're looking for, what they hope will happen and what kind of medicine they think they want, if they've had different ones. Frequently they know just what they want to take, and we've already got the standard dosage for that person. Fine. We put it in an envelope, until we've gotten everybody.

We all gather in the living room again and we have our dropping ceremony, which is a very nice ceremony. After everybody's dropped, they wander around, they're quiet. We ask them to still be quiet, until they feel themselves starting to turn on. Before that they've staked out tripping spaces, which may or may not be different from the sleeping spaces. If there's two people coming together as a couple we want them to trip in different parts of the house, whereas they might have slept together.

When they start to turn on, they go to their pads, lie down, put the eyeshades on and the earphones on and there's music playing already. They just lay there until they turn on. The only time we ever hear from them is when somebody feels they haven't turned on and want a booster. They'll call one of us over. Or if they have to get up and pee later on. We've got it down now so we know everybody's dosage, so we rarely have to give a booster. They lay on their pads, and we're in the kitchen sitting and talking and all that stuff and waiting, just being available.

Myron: All the time they're really in it, they're laying there listening to music?

Jacob: Right.

Myron: You don't encourage any interrelationship.

Jacob: No! We don't want anybody to talk. Sometimes, somebody when they have MDMA, Jesus Christ, you know, they want to hold hands, it's so loving and all that. That's all right. If somebody doesn't want to hold hands, they're on a different material, all they have to do is hold their hand back and everybody respects their position. The MDMA people like to get up and do some hugging and then we set them right back down. We'll all hug them, they'll call us over just for a big hug. They're so full of love, it's really fantastically beautiful.

By middle afternoon they start coming down and they start moving around. They'll go outside in the patio or just sit around in the house and they're still turned on or coming down, whatever. Later on there are some things put out on the table—salad, some crackers and some fruit and some things for nibbles. Then when they're all down, when they're all down enough so that they're quite functional, we all gather in the living room and we have our champagne ceremony. All of this is tradition that's built up over the years. It's hard for me to trace all the different activities that we went through to get to this point. But this seems to be the most fruitful. The old timers who come back to trip with us once in a while who went through that early stuff say this is a helluva lot better way to trip.

After the champagne ceremony we have dinner. After dinner, we'll all sit around and laugh and giggle and tell jokes and have fun, or sit quietly and just observe the others that are still tripping. Or if they want to be alone they go off somewhere to keep going on their trip. The music continues so they can listen to it if they want to, until they're ready to go to bed. When they're ready to go to bed they find an empty pad and lay down. There's no staking out because they're pretty stoned. They get up in the morning oh, by 7:30 anyway. We have breakfast at nine. We ask them to be quiet again in the morning, too, because their trip is still going on even though they're not stoned. After breakfast they all gather in the living room again.

And the leader usually has a reading. I always had a reading, it's a nice thing, very appropriate, no matter what the hell you do, it's appropriate. From where they're at, everything's appropriate. They go around again and they talk about what happened.

One of the last things that's said on Friday night—it's traditional, too—"I want you all to now take a look at yourselves, close your eyes and look at yourself and just see what you're experiencing now, that's all. Just see what you're experiencing now." They give them about a minute to do that and then the leader says, "We'll ask you to do this again on Sunday morning." And he does.

This sharing is the high point of the trip for everybody. Not only have they had their trip, they're going to have ten other people's or eleven other people's trips, too. And the *feeling* and the *sharing* and the talking out of where they are, sometimes the deep crying that comes out. Everybody is just pulled into it. And we *are* one. Until then we do not know what happened on anybody's trip. We don't know! That's our payoff for having been there all that time and handling it like we do. When they're all through we have lunch and we get ready to leave. By mid-afternoon they go home. They sign up for the next one they want to come to. They are available every month.

Myron: So if you only have it once a month and you can only handle ten to twelve, probably you have a much larger group moving in and out of the group experience.

Jacob: Oh, yes! Oh, yes!

Myron: What would you say is sort of a working number?

Jacob: The active members of the group are about 40 or 50 who are coming every third or fourth month. There are about 100 who come less frequently. Something like that. You see, we have a priority list. The priority list is this. First trippers have first priority, the first time they're coming to the group. The second priority is somebody who hasn't tripped for a long time. Third priority is somebody who is in some kind of space where they really need a trip, want very much to have a trip, and we agree that it would be a good thing for them to have it, if there isn't a possibility for them to have it another way. But they don't generally want to the other way, they'd rather trip with the group anyway. And then there's another priority: we try to keep a balance between men and women.

Well, that fills the group, you see, if we get through all of those priorities.

CHAPTER V

MATERIALS AND DOSES

MYRON: I AM INTERESTED in the different chemicals that you've run across. What kind of significant differences, if any, do you see among the different agents?

Jacob: We have a spectrum of materials that we use. They've been screened out. I've tried many of them, explored many of the new ones that have come out. I'll list the ones that are most suitable for a group trip as far as we're concerned. There are many more but most of them will do the same thing as these do and most of them won't do as well as these do.

One of them is LSD. Everyone first has an individual trip with me which establishes their LSD dose level. Other materials we use are the Psilocybe cubensis mushroom, dried. And mescaline—we don't use peyote. MDA. Ibogaine. Harmaline—we call it *yage*. It's the active ingredient of *yage*, that's the harmaline hydrochloride.[1] MDMA, Adam.[2] I have not adopted 2C-B. It just doesn't seem suitable for a group trip at all. Or DOB or the TMA series. TMA-2[3] is the one that was thought best for an experience.

Myron: I'm surprised that DOB hasn't worked well.

Jacob: We've tried it, and some of them will say, "Yeah, it was a nice trip but I get more out of or I'd rather have__." It doesn't do anything more for me than one of these others. I like to keep it down to just a few.

---

1. Harmaline is called *yage* in error. It is not the active ingredient in *yage*. DMT and/or other tryptamines are. See Ott. *Pharmacotheon*. Kennewick, WA: Natural Products Co. 1993, page 260. footnote 3.

2. The code name "Adam" for MDMA was a term coined by Jacob.

3. For a description of these compounds, see Shulgin, A. T. & A. Shulgin, *PIHKAL*, Berkeley, CA: Transform Press, 1991.

Different Kinds of Trips

There's the *psychedelic* trip and the *psychoactive* trip. The psychedelics are the acid, mescaline, psilocybin. Visions and hallucinations and things like that. That's what characterizes the psychedelics. These three are psychoactive, but there are other psychoactives that are not psychedelic—MDA, harmaline, and ibogaine. Some people see colors and some visions on those.

Harmaline

I would put that in the psychedelic one rather than just the psychoactive one without the psychedelic because we don't take it alone, nobody takes it alone. It takes a helluva lot to turn on and you get so God damned sick if you took enough to turn on that it's horrible. We take it with acid or psilocybin and it puts a new dimension on the acid trip. Very primitive, you get right down to the primitive side of yourself. The men who take it find their real masculinity and the women who take it find their true femininity. As a matter of fact, some Indians when they take *yage* and they have their religious ceremonies, the men take it separate in their own hogan, and the women take it separate in their own hogan. They do not mix, because for the women, it's a woman's medicine, and for the men it's a man's medicine. Same medicine.

Myron: On the psychoactive list, would you put MDMA on that list also?

Jacob: Yes. That's Adam. Right. It's not a hallucinogen. The hallucinogens give visions, colors, and new dimensions to all of the senses, like hearing, vision, music—you know, music is a trip and that's for all three of those. Hallucinations are very characteristic of course with eyes closed or eyes open, it doesn't matter. That's what I meant when I said visions. In some ways, people will say that they have a more spiritual trip on the hallucinogens because they see very important visions, spiritual visions in some sense to them. It's all an individual experience and their own reaction to it. The most popular one for that is psilocybin. It's a more spiritual trip. People will say that, although they'll also say that it's a spiritual trip on mescaline and acid. Now we'll go to the others, like MDA.

Myron: Just before we leave that, there's another thing. I don't know if you've read much by Gerald Heard. He talks about analytical thinking versus integral thinking, and with the hallucinogens—and maybe this is what you're calling visions, too—somehow you seem to jump up to a higher level of understanding where things seem to fall into place and relatedness more clearly.

Jacob: Oh, yes. That happens definitely on the hallucinogenic trips. Very clearly. That's part of the transformation.

Myron: Higher conceptualization?

Jacob: Conceptualization—most people would object to that, because it's not a conceptual process.

Myron: Maybe realization.

Jacob: Realization. Experiencing in a new dimension. And, coming out of a very deep level of feeling. I prefer feeling to emotion, although emotions will accompany it. Crying and things. Again, the word that I would use now is a realization of the truth. *THE TRUTH.* God's truth. Not the one we think is truth. Not of the mind. It's of the Self. The soul. Everything you see that you experience you experience with a whole new configuration.

MDA

Psychoactive, very clear, answers questions, MDA clarifies your life, puts everything in a correct perspective for you, tells you what you are doing that is satisfying, what you can do that will be more satisfying. You come out with a *good* feeling about yourself. It helps you to see all your difficulties in a different light, and they cease to be difficulties. You become aware of the fact that everything is happening just exactly the way it should be happening, and you're doing everything you *need* to do. Just relax and go do it! This is pretty characteristic, at least with the first trip with MDA. Subsequent ones, too. It's a great experience for relating people to each other—yeah, you have a good feeling about yourself and the world around you. It brings you into the experience of the moment. That's the greatest material for learning that lesson. There's nothing but the moment, and that experience brings it home *very well.*

I remember one trip that I had, every time that I'd get anxious the trip would tell me, "Everything is in this moment, nothing exists except this moment. There you are. This is what exists." Every time I would get anxious I would say, "Hey, wait a minute! I'm anxious! What was I thinking about just then?" What I was thinking about was before or after or about to or whatever. I wasn't in the moment. I said, "See, you're not here in the moment." I'd look around and I'd experience with my senses and the anxiety disappeared. It's a great lesson to have. That's MDA.

Ibogaine

Ibogaine is something else. It's similar. All of these have certain qualities that are common to all of them. Also, no hallucinations. It's a heavier trip. A deeper and a longer trip, and for many people it takes longer to turn on. It's a very profound trip for everybody but people experience it differently. Some people love it, they love the lessons that they get from it. Some people find it a very painful experience. Those who find it painful are the ones who have not been confronting what Mr. Ibogaine is handing them and have been trying to avoid it.

You asked me once before something about confronting blocks. This is a place where people will confront blocks, as a matter of fact, if they have been unwilling to accept them or believe them or often try to deny them. A truth that they're trying to deny. Mr. Ibogaine won't let you do that. You can fuck it up if you want to. But nobody wants to. You have a great respect for Mr. Ibogaine. You experience it. Great respect. You listen to it. You may not do anything about it but you'll know that this is true. This is so. Yeah.

MDMA

And then of course MDMA. *Beautiful* trip. Just full of beauty and love and good feeling and acceptance of your self and realization of your own perfection in such a way that you say, "I don't think I ever want to put myself down or find myself wrong, because I'm not wrong. I'm being guided all of the time." It brings that into an experience.

Dose Levels

Jacob: Nobody can come to the group trip until they've first had a trip with me. I've already established the level it takes for them to turn on with acid. All first trips are acid. Even if they've had 500 acid trips before that. Suppose they have a full trip on 250 micrograms. All right, then 250 is their dose level. It could be more. I generally start at 250 unless I have a reason to think that they're more sensitive and don't need that much.

Sometimes 250 isn't enough, I'll give them another 125 micrograms. If that isn't enough I'll give them another 125. I keep building it up gradually until they really are turned on. They may have to have 500 to turn on. Some people have to go up to 750 to turn on. Hard heads, I call them. If they started out at 250 and ended up with 500, I'll call their base level 375 micrograms, halfway between 250 and 500 because by the time I gave them the second booster they've already dissipated a certain amount, they don't need more. That's the base level, and the base level for acid in general becomes the thing that I compare all the others with.

When they come in for the group trip we talk and decide what they're going to take. They want to know what's available, what kind of trip it is, what happens on a trip. They don't know what to do because they haven't had any experience with it. I generally suggest a second one to try. They may want to have another acid trip or they want to have a psilocybin trip or something like that, because they've heard about it. We'll talk about it and we agree on a format, and *I* decide on the dosage they're going to have, because I have something to compare it with and they don't have.

Frequently now, more frequently than anything else, I suggest MDA for the second trip. I tell them, "It's a very different kind of trip. It's not like your other one was. It's also a very, very good trip for you." And they say, "Okay. I'll take your word for it."

If they take 250 micrograms of acid to turn on we start them on 150 milligrams of MDA. Most of the time that's enough. After an hour, if they're not turned on, I'll give a 50 milligram booster. Most of the times that'll turn them on. If it doesn't turn them on in thirty minutes I'll give another 50 milligram booster. On this trip they'll establish their base for MDA. There are variables between people, you know, and also variables with the same material with the same person from one time to another. But this is the general picture.

Okay, they've had that trip. Then they come in and want to try another, a different kind of material. I'll suggest either psilocybin, which is hallucinogenic, because a lot of them *love* the visions and things like that or mescaline. Ibogaine is much later. I like for them to have that after they've had the others. Ibogaine is about the last one I have them try. It's a progressive, one, ibogaine. Each trip brings you to another level.

Myron: How much psilocybin do you give?

Jacob: Three grams of the mushroom is equivalent to 250 micrograms of acid. If they took 375 micrograms of acid, we'd give them 4.5 grams of the mushroom.

Myron: It's a pretty direct correlation?

Jacob: Pretty direct. Yeah.

Myron: And how much mescaline would correlate to 250 micrograms of acid?

Jacob: Most people don't really turn on with less than 500 milligrams. We don't do mescaline very much because it's very expensive and they seem to get as much out of the acid or psilocybin as the mescaline. Nothing special comes to them on mescaline.

MDMA

The first time they take MDMA I give them 150 milligrams. Sometimes that does it for them. If it doesn't, then I give them a 50 booster. After that we establish their base. Then I know that it takes 200. The maximum I'll give is 300, although there's one person who takes 300 and a booster of 200 after he's started coming down. It doesn't hurt him. Doesn't hurt his heart or anything like that. I don't feel comfortable giving them more than 300. If they haven't turned on I say, "You take what you've got and that's it." And you know, when they find out they can't have a booster they lay down and the sons of bitches they turn on! (Much laughter.)

I've had quite a thing about this business of boosters. I've had lots of hassles about it, because they want to really blast through. Sometimes they'll get close but they can't get through and they want to blast through. They think more medicine will do it. I tell them this every time we have a session, "More is not better. Lay down and stay down. No wandering around, because as soon as you start to be functional you detract. You've got to get into your ego to be functional. Lay down and have your whole trip and when you're all the way down, really coming down, then you can get up and walk around. Or if you have to go to the bathroom one of us will help you go to the bathroom." Or something like that. That's very important.

Harmaline

Harmaline goes with either acid or psilocybin. I generally give them 125 milligrams. I used to give them 250 milligrams and they'd get pretty damned nauseated by it. The 125 milligrams is sufficient for them. This is a psychoactive material but it's not psychedelic, and this amount does not add to the base level. They would take their normal amount of acid and just add this which does not increase the activity of the other psychedelic. It's just an auxiliary, and brings a different dimension to it. Some people would prefer 250 milligrams instead of 125 milligrams of the harmaline. Those who have trouble with nausea take it anally.

Myron: You just put a capsule up their rectum?

Jacob: Yep! You just say, "Squat, find your asshole, put the capsule right up your asshole, shove it up as far as you can. Go like that." (Demonstrates.) That always gets a nice laugh.

Ibogaine

Myron: That leaves ibogaine, then.

Jacob: This we have to explore to find the right dose. If I'm not sure how much it takes to turn them on, then I give them three capsules. A capsule is 75 milligrams of ibogaine, the active ingredient. It's a half-gram capsule, it's a pretty big capsule. But the active ingredient is 75 milligrams of ibogaine. I give them three. That's about 225 milligrams. If they don't turn on after an hour or hour and a half at the most, we give them a fourth one, and they'll turn on with that. Few of them need more than that. It's hard on the body, too. I don't want them to take more if they don't need it.

They've established their bases. If they didn't turn on with three then I know that four is necessary. Sometimes I give them four and it was much too much and they know it. I mean they had too much. It was the proper amount according to the way that I grade it but it was too much of this particular medicine for this particular person. Next time I'll give them three.

Some people do two. Some people get a little trip on one. Very rare, but they do. A mild trip. That's the idea.

Myron: Don't some people want to start with one and work their way up?

Jacob: Not any more. I used to do that. I tried it a couple of times, it doesn't work. I start with three. If three's too much you go back to two the next time. If three isn't enough then you go to four this time and you start with four next time.

I have a record of what everybody's taken, and how many boosters and how long into the trip they had to have the booster. It helps me to determine what to do. They learn themselves what their schedule is.

Okay, that's it for materials and dosages and kinds of trips.

CHAPTER VI

OUTCOMES

MYRON: WHAT WE MIGHT talk about now is you've had this large number of people who have come to you and have had individual trips and group trips. Could we talk about some of the kinds of changes that you've seen in people as a result of this?

Jacob: You know that's a very difficult thing to do. The only thing I can do at the moment is to recall what they were like when they first came to me, and then to see them as they are now—beautiful loving friends of mine out there in the world doing great things. Really doing great things. All of them. And continuously on the path of further exploring and further searching. I always try everything that comes along. When something comes along that I try that is very fruitful to me and could be fruitful to my people, I let them know about it. And they go do it. If they find something that's really good they let me know about it, and I go do it.

Your question now: "Can you say what happened to them?" One of the first things that they learn to do is to take complete responsibility for themselves and their lives. This is something that we *all* keep working on *all the time*. More and more and more. No more blaming. No more attributing the cause of anything out there to anybody else. That's really the *heart of the whole training* that I'm involved in. You could describe it in one sentence, that's it.

There's many manifestations, many ways that you can go about it. The people change from a very disturbed, mixed-up state to a clear place where they function much more creatively, in terms of relations to themselves and outside. They affect the lives of everybody they come in contact with in a positive way for the most part, whereas before they affected them negatively. They gave them trouble. They are much more satisfied with themselves. And they are committed to the process, to the growth process, to continually exploring. This is true for most of the people I've worked with. Some have drifted off, I don't know what else to say. It's not their bag right now.

Myron: How about sensory enhancement?

Jacob: Yeah, our eyes become open! It's like the Garden of Eden. Our eyes become open, and our senses. We're much more aware, much more acutely aware. For food, that happens. Especially right after the trip. You fall back in your old ways all the time, too.

You're trying to find out whatever I've discovered about different kinds of outcomes from tripping. Transformation is the only word that will fit. From one way of looking at things to another one, whatever they're looking at. I always tell my people, it's one of my favorite statements: Nobody has ever been able to achieve transformation by their own unaided efforts. This is a belief that I have. It requires some sort of a medium. The medium can be a medicine, the medium can be alcohol, the medium can be transformation of consciousness. Could be a deep crisis in their lives. Could be a priest or a minister or a psychotherapist as the facilitator. It could be something that they smoked, it could be some one of thousands of things that grow that they would ingest that turn them on. Turning on is the phrase that I use now for getting into a state where transformation occurs.

But just by sitting there and trying to do it, I don't know if anybody else has done it. Even Milarepa. He did it by sitting for a number of years in a cave meditating. Sensory deprivation. I think that's the best word that we have that tells what happens on an LSD trip. They've taken blood samples from people who have been in that meditative state and from people in the middle of a trip and they find that the changes in the blood are very similar. The serotonin content of the blood and I don't know all about that chemical stuff. I'm not good on the chemical stuff. The same things, the same results come. The visions that they have.

Myron: I'm curious about the progression that people make with these different materials. First they start with LSD and then possibly when they join the group they'll repeat that or try psilocybin and then you recommend MDA...

Jacob: If they're doing all right we'll talk about the different materials and the kinds of trips they may choose or they may say, "I don't know, I don't have any basis for choosing." So we'll say, "Well, try this. This is usually the next one that people take."

Myron: And after MDA then maybe you'll have them try Adam.

Jacob: No. Another psychedelic with *yage*. We try to get them through the spectrum of things as soon as we can so that they know which ones to choose.

Myron: Then after *yage* maybe MDMA.

Jacob: Well, psilocybin. It may take a year or so before they've gone through the spectrum. There's also tripping at home, too; people will do that with other group members. They'll have a little group combine and have a trip with somebody sitting with them, so they have other chances to trip once they've been a member of the group.

Myron: Once they've been exposed to the whole spectrum, is there any kind of weighting? What is the popularity distribution of the different things? Are there any particular favorites?

Jacob: Adam is definitely first, MDMA is first. It depends on where they're at and what kind of trip they want. If they haven't got anything special they may just want to have Adam again because it's such a beautiful trip. If they've got things they want to work on they'll take a psychedelic, or they'll take MDA or something like that. We don't use much MDA any more. A work trip is a *yage* trip or an ibogaine trip where they've got things to work out.

Myron: Do you have any feelings about what each of these things are specifically best for? You did give me that.

Jacob: Mostly there is much more likenesses between them all than there is differences. They all turn you on, they all bring you back to your center.

Myron: I am a little surprised at your initial dose because that seems higher than what some people use as an introduction. I guess really what you're providing are very profound experiences and you're really pretty focused and oriented to make sure that they get the most profound kind of experience.

Jacob: Right. And it goes very smoothly, because it's a routine kind of thing. Yet it draws my attention, holds my energy, and all of that.

I really wasn't aware of how much energy went into this kind of thing until I stopped, really started cutting down. It took me two to three days to recuperate, because it takes one hell of a lot of energy out of a person.

Myron: I wanted to ask you, with individual sessions, too, do you find it tiring?

Jacob: Oh you, damned right! *Absolutely.* I don't schedule anything for the next day, as I'm very tired the next day. When I come home from the thing I just plop into bed. Even though I'm sitting still all the time! And I'm reading! You know, keeping my mind interested, but there's a draw of energy that's fabulous.

Myron: I thought it was the most tiring thing a person could do. I probably had problems where I was probably too involved, but I know our Medical Director quit sitting with people just as soon as he had others who would do it.

Jacob: I was very involved in the very beginning. Now I'm not that way involved.

Myron: Do you find that you're less tired?

Jacob: No. No. I'm still very tired.

Myron: It takes a lot of energy.

Jacob: Yes indeed. I'm still very tired. But I don't get emotionally involved with them. I don't cry when they're crying and when they experience something I don't identify with it. I just sit there quietly and I'm aware of what's going on and when they start to cry or when they're doing something that indicates where they're at in their trip I say, "That's great, oh, fine, stay with it, kid." Something like that.

Myron: It must be enormously satisfying. Even with the little bit of work that I have been involved in there's nothing more satisfying than when another person makes these discoveries.

Jacob: Right. It's what I said earlier, there's nothing more satisfying than turning somebody on to themselves. At the end of a weekend when I'd see what fantastic things have happened to these people, I'd say, "Whatever I've had to go through, it's *worth* it to produce these results!"

See Appendix I for examples of personal accounts.

FINALE

It is now sixteen years since these interviews were conducted. Simply rereading them has brought back the richness of these encounters, and an immense appreciation of the expanded vistas that psychedelics make possible to the earnest explorer. They support and confirm a wealth of additional accounts given by other researchers.[1]

Immersed in the impact of this work, it seems to me incomprehensible that our society has sunk so deeply into unconsciousness as to be unaware of such possibilities. The general public, unfamiliar with the power of our minds, remains for the most part locked in mass hypnotism, secured within the self-constructed walls that lock out the prodigious possibilities of life, the joy and exuberance waiting to be claimed. Our birthright of wisdom and compassion has been sacrificed on the altar of self-interest, materialism, and reductionism. So opposed are we to discovering the errors of our decisions that we have made practically all substances which can reveal to us our true nature illegal to possess.

Nothing would have pleased Jacob more than to know that the telling of his story has helped our society understand that there are powerful tools available for self realization—that vast new possibilities in life await us when we take on the responsibility of making these new tools available and learn how to use them. We will then recognize Jacob as a true pioneer and dedicated servant of humanity.

1. For example, see: Adamson, S. *Through the Gateway of the Heart.* San Francisco: Four Trees Publications, 1985. Shulgin, A. T. & A. Shulgin, *PIHKAL.* Berkeley, CA: Transform Press, 1991. Stolaroff, M. J. *Thanatos to Eros: Thirty-five Years of Psychedelic Exploration.* Berlin: VWB-Yerlag fur Wissenschaft und Bildung, 1994. Available from Thaneros Press.

EPILOGUE

THE LAST TRIP: PEACEFUL CLOSURE FOR JACOB

ALEXANDER SHULGIN

MY FIRST MEMORIES OF JACOB were back in the early days of the Berkeley scene, during the time of the free speech vigor. No, my first meeting with him actually preceded all of that, and even preceded the Berkeley Barb being peddled by bearded hippies on every street corner all the way up Telegraph Avenue from Dwight Way to Sather Gate. As I remember, it even preceded the tear gas and the helicopters of law and order. Pre-People's Park. Pre-Doctor Hippocrates. Pre-Mario Savio. Jacob and I would agree to meet at our favorite cafe on the Avenue and share an espresso (a new fad just introduced from Italy) and discuss just how to get the pink color out of crystalline MDA. I had no idea, and had never asked where the MDA had come from, nor why it was pink. Jacob never told me. But I suggested washing it with ether containing a bit of acetone, and the pink color apparently went away. This was in the pre-MDMA era, when MDA (the "Mellow Drug of America," sometimes called the "love drug") was very much the favorite of the therapists and the psychedelic explorers of the time. It had been kosherized, after all, by being promoted by one of the largest pharmaceutical houses in the United States (Smith, Kline, and French) after having been discovered and espoused by an eminent Professor of Pharmacology (Dr. Gordon A. Alles, from UCLA).

I was not particularly interested in MDA, as I had my own acaulescent world of phenethylamine relatives that was going in all directions at once. And Jacob was not particularly interested in my manic and broad diffusion of new compounds as he had his MDA which was a familiar and, for him, completely predictable tool. A decade or two later,

I caught his attention with the material MDMA, but that story is the stuff of a chapter in another book. I would, here, rather talk about quite a different material, mescaline. This remarkable alkaloid demands a special place in my notes as it was the first psychedelic I had ever tried. And, it commanded an equally special place in Jacob's notes, as it was the last of his experiences.

I, and a number of my friends, had found a time for communion and exploration, and mescaline was the chosen vehicle for the day. Jacob accepted 300 milligrams of the sulfate salt in water solution, wished us well, and drank it down. As did we all. In a half hour he retreated towards the bathroom (nausea is a rather dependable companion under such circumstances), then he chose to lie down by himself in a back bedroom. I searched him out in another hour, but he indicated that he wished to remain alone for a while yet.

An hour later he rejoined us, with a humorous yet wistful smile on his face, and told us that he had pretty much decided that this was it. He had had it. "Too much nausea?" I asked. "No," he replied. "It isn't until I have gotten sick and urped that I know I have turned on." "So what is this 'it' that you have had it with?" I asked him.

He sat down in a soft, comfy chair, and looked at me, and smiled. "I think that I have found my place of peace. I know that I will live until I die, and I don't have to rush it, and I don't have to keep proving that I still have piles of life left to explore. I'm getting too old to try to demonstrate to others that I'm young and still learning. So I'll just let things be. What's to prove?"

He sat there for the next couple of hours, watching all the others exchanging dynamic interplays of ideas, opinions, and clever conversation. All this was not directed towards him, but was simply cast adrift in the air about him. He listened, and that infinitely peaceful smile never once left his face. I suddenly realized that some day I, too, would be an observer of the passing scene rather than a participant in it.

A few hours later, as we all sat around a fabulous chicken casserole with some acceptable white wine, I asked him if he had had a rewarding trip today. He told me he had, indeed, been "out there" for a while, and that now he was back with us he thought he would probably stay here, in this reality, for his remaining days. He had closed his circle. He was together.

I hope that someday I will experience the completion and the integration that I saw, that day, in Jacob's face. At that future moment, I just might discover that I too have become a complete person.

APPENDIX I: PERSONAL ACCOUNTS

THE RESULTS OF the author's in-depth interviews with five different individuals who have gone through the program described in this book are summarized in these personal accounts. The information was mostly prompted by questions asked of the individual participants. Assumed names are assigned in each case.

A word about the questions. Those of a scientific mind would no doubt like to see the questionnaire that was used for these interviews. As a matter of fact, it was my intent to develop a questionnaire that could be filled out by all the participants, and I would summarize the results by analyzing the answers.

Jacob objected very much to this, as did others who had extensive experience with persons going through this program. The problem is that these experiences are such expansive openers, and lead into so many dimensions of understanding and experience that it is quite restricting to attempt to channel the results into the narrow ruts of a preconceived set of questions. The attempt to do so is limiting and frustrating to the person being interviewed.

Consequently, I armed myself with a checklist to make sure I covered areas of interest, and at the same time encouraged the participant to relate what they found to be most interesting and valuable. In this way I hoped to capture important areas of functioning, while allowing the participant to communicate more fully the extent of her or his experience.

ROBERT

Robert is in his early forties, unmarried, and works as a commissioned salesman. He first became drawn to psychedelics through reading about them. After he participated in his first psychedelic session, he continued with one experience per month for eleven months. By the time of this interview, he had completed seventy-five to eighty psychedelic sessions, ten of these on his own. The compounds which he has experienced include MDMA, ibogaine, LSD, LSD with harmaline, peyote, mushrooms, MDA, and 2C-B.[1]

When Robert became aware of a program that used psychedelics therapeutically, he entered it. His sense of adventure played a part in motivating him to participate. He was also motivated by his yearning for an experience of God, feeling that this was an important aspect of life that he was missing. In addition, there were a number of things about himself that he was not happy with and that he hoped to change through the therapeutic use of psychedelics.

In Robert's first session, he ingested three grams of mushrooms. He felt his female companion became a leopard woman. When they reached out and touched, red energy passed between their hands like a neon light. Later in the afternoon he found that everything was gorgeous. His first group experience was with ibogaine, where he had very rich and enjoyable interior visions for many hours.

During a memorable experience in which he took a combination of LSD and harmaline, Robert found the power within himself to feel his strength and explore his masculinity. He found himself to be fearless and a powerhouse of energy. During this session Robert felt strong like a leopard and was able to overcome his fear of snakes.

After his second most significant session, a powerful experience with 2C-B, he felt that he had "cleansed his lenses"; the world looked different, like washing a muddy car. A heightened sensory awareness stayed with him after this session, and opened him up to and was extended by a subsequent MDMA session.

---

1. 4-Bromo-2,5-Dim ethoxyphenethylamine, a new chemical that was investigated for a while, then abandoned because of the variability in response and the fact that it did not lend itself.

Robert describes an experience with MDMA as his most profound psychedelic session. The session began with the ingestion of 150 milligrams of MDMA. After one and a half hours, he had not noticed any effects so he ingested 75 more milligrams as a booster. This first booster did not achieve the desired effect so a second booster of 50 milligrams was reluctantly administered. Even after being administered a second booster his experience had not started. Robert asked for another booster but his request was denied. He was told perhaps it was about time that he had a nothing trip. Three hours after the beginning of the session he had a profound experience of God which he describes as the most joyous moment of his life. A month later he was still happy, joyous, grateful, and completely satisfied.

Robert attributes many of the positive changes in his life to his psychedelic therapy. Of the benefits he reported, the most outstanding has been that of profoundly experiencing God within himself. Before he had these psychedelic experiences, Robert had rejected Christianity and had no feeling for the existence of God. He has since joined the Unity Church and attends services, which have become the highlight of his week. He is now engrossed in reading spiritual books, listening to music, looking at nature, with gratitude at the beauty of the world welling out to God every day. He has not undertaken any new formal education, but has greatly increased his reading and study through the Unity Church.

The overall quality of the relationships in Robert's life has improved. He now feels more relaxed around people, more in the present. He has dropped some of his shyness, and is less clinging. He has discovered that he essentially loves his mother, whom he had felt was a very difficult person. His experiences have allowed him to keep relationships going despite resentments. He feels an ability to experience love, which he had not done for years.

When dealing with the world at large, Robert no longer feels the need to be constantly on the lookout, scanning for danger. The fear of danger has now fallen away. His fear of death and anxiety levels have also diminished.

There has been a significant change in Robert's relationship to his work. He has dropped an old, stressful job and has taken a job based on commission. Previously he was much too rigid and anxious to consider a job where income was uncertain. Robert has also experienced a change in his recreational activities due to his psychedelic therapy sessions. His appreciation of nature and his love of music have increased. He has abandoned his television set, acquired a huge record collection, and reports a greater interest in reading, particularly metaphysical books. After sessions, he often has spontaneous flows of writing.

The detrimental effects that Robert has experienced have been occasional feelings of paranoia. One of these experiences began with a group session in which he had taken a peyote extract and mushrooms. The initial dose did not achieve the desired effects, so Robert took a booster. The first part of the experience was pleasant, but in the afternoon he turned quite paranoid. This feeling lasted for a week, until a solo experience with MDMA erased it.

Robert had another bout with paranoia when he ingested 100 micrograms of LSD with a friend. In this instance, talking it through with his friend cleared about eighty percent of his paranoid feelings. Robert also experienced paranoid feelings for a period of close to three months after his 2C-B encounter; however, he felt that this experience laid the groundwork for his magnificent MDMA journey. On another note, though his intuition has increased somewhat and there are times at work when he gets a sudden flash of understanding, his energy level has gone downhill. He finds it hard to get started in the morning. This is sometimes disturbing. He thinks it may be aging.

Overall, Robert reported a great improvement in the quality of his life because of his psychedelic therapy sessions. All of his experiences have contributed to this, but the MDMA experience was the most outstanding, with the 2C-B experience next. He can better appreciate the beauty in the world and God plays an important role in his life. One of the greatest gains is the contact with the group, sharing experiences. These relations are now the richest part of his life. Through his psychedelic therapy sessions, Robert has gained innumerable insights about himself and the world in which he lives.

SUSAN

Susan is 34 and a freelance graphic artist. When she learned of the program of psychedelic therapy, she immediately wished to participate (3-1/2 years previous to this interview). She has had approximately 40 experiences, about half of which were on her own. She has used LSD, LSD and harmaline,

MDA, MDMA, ibogaine, mescaline, 2C-B, and mushrooms. She entered this program looking for a booster in life and to further develop the progress made through another personal growth program.

Susan has had a number of outstanding experiences with psychedelics. Some very dramatic ones have occurred with ibogaine, her favorite material. She finds that ibogaine forces you to look at what you have placed between yourself and love and that you have no choice; it will not let go of you until you are redeemed. Many people do not like it but she finds that the best thing to do is "confront your crap rather than laying around in paradise." She always feels best after experiences in which she has confronted fear.

Before one ibogaine experience, Susan had set herself up for a perfect boyfriend where she would function out of love with no projections. She took up with the boyfriend of her best girlfriend after the two broke up. Her girlfriend returned after thirty days and reunited with her old boyfriend, which hurt Susan very deeply.

She took ibogaine and went through cycles of resentment, fear, anger, and sadness for hours and hours, over and over again. It wouldn't stop. At the end of the day, she sat up and decided that at least she could get up and go to the bathroom. She suddenly experienced her head filled with light. For the next half hour, she felt like the Buddha, a most beautiful experience. Her conclusion is that Mr. Ibogaine does not let go of you until he is through with you.

During another ibogaine session, she thought knives were hidden everywhere and she was filled with murderous thoughts. She saw Jesus being crucified and finally drove in the nails herself. After hours and hours of experiencing Christ crucified, she realized that Jesus forgave her despite her abominable act, and that He also forgave Judas. She then reached a sense of Cosmic Consciousness, One Mind, and the knowledge that God was real. At another time, she took MDMA and had a glowing experience. A week later with ibogaine, she asked why life could not be like the MDMA experience all the time. The answer came quickly, "Because of fear." She thought she now had the answer and was through, but a voice said to her, "No you don't!" She was then forced to experience fear in every conceivable way. She kept trying to hide but was unable to, so she finally gave up. The experience was horrible, with much yelling. She described the most comfortable she could feel was to have one million razor blades stuck into her body and have them explode. She saw no hope and finally gave up and collapsed on a pad. She was then filled with a channel of white light and felt reborn. Beauty came, and there was pure, exquisite tension between fear and beauty. She did one of her best designs after this experience.

In her personal growth pursuits, Susan felt her biggest decision was to stop making herself miserable. Before, her energy was hyper and frantic and she felt she wasn't "home." Now she realizes that she can be still, rather than constantly chasing after activities. She is willing to make peace with the past, allow herself to feel depressed sometimes, and look inside herself for her real intention.

The biggest benefit of Susan's psychedelic therapy has been freeing herself of projections. She used to project onto everything. In her relationships, she would fall in love, project all over her partner, and drive herself crazy. She has since learned to ask herself what she really wants and has discovered that love is not "out there" to be found, but comes from within yourself; you don't need to go running after it.

Interestingly, Susan reports that she stopped wearing glasses. She feels that she doesn't need them because her vision has improved. She is more aware of detail and color and is less distracted. She can become absorbed in the beauty of simple things, like the reflection of lights from waves on the surface of water.

In the area of sensitivity, she finds herself more open, not as defensive, and has dropped fears and judgments. It is much easier for her to make close contact with people in everyday affairs such as clerks in stores.

In terms of her creativity, Susan reports that her graphics have gotten "very clean in design." She finds that after confronting her fears in experiences she does her best designs. A significant change took place in her work activity. She was a supervisor for a while, and went through a period of attempting to make her department very efficient, eliminate sloppiness, and "get on the ball." She wanted to run things in a regimented manner, but no one was interested. In pondering the problem, it came to her to attempt not so much to control her co-workers but to relax her stranglehold on them and trust the process. In finally deciding to "let them do what they want," relations immediately improved—the employees were happier, and things operated more efficiently. Susan had been very resentful of her mother and father, despite having been given everything. She previously saw herself as a "snotty little kid" resenting authority and wanting to grow up immediately. In her first psychedelic session, she realized the contribution her parents had made to her life, and totally flipped in her attitude. She forgave them even though there was nothing to forgive, and the relationship has been wonderful ever since. In addition to the renewed relationship with her parents and the continued easy, open relationship with her three sisters, she now has a whole new set of friends, mostly those from the group psychedelic experiences, who now feel closer than her own family.

The biggest change in her life regarding her conduct with other people has been learning to mind her own business. She has found it best not to sympathize or empathize with others to help them get over hurts, but simply to tell the truth and mind her own business. This is working very well.

Susan at first had a strong feeling that she had to help save the world. Despite volunteering eight hours a day on top of an eight hour job, she was compulsive and felt guilty that she was not doing enough. She now feels that whatever you do makes a difference; what is important is how you do it rather than what you do. She feels that working on herself is making a contribution to the planet. Since all minds are one, one day there will be enough clear minds to achieve a mass world improvement.

Susan has had some incredible experiences of God, or the One Mind of Cosmic Consciousness. Susan found that her own energy was insignificant compared to that of God. She learned that if she was stuck in an experience and was thrashing around, the answer was not to go looking for God but to realize that God is inside and to come from God. She has had some profound biblical-type experiences. The implications of these experiences for herself are to remove her own barriers and make decisions, take responsibility for herself, tell the truth as far as she knows it, and to understand that being willing is what frees one.

The only detrimental effect that Susan reported is that sometimes she would be tired for a couple of days after a session. There have been no long-range adverse effects.

DICK

Dick is 33 and has been married nine years. He owns and operates a stained glass business with his wife and another woman as partners. He had used psychedelics previously to entering this program, but mostly for recreation. His experiences were meaningless, had no direction, and he got nothing from them. Dick had about ten experiences before entering the program and has had ten to twelve experiences subsequently, starting about one year before this interview. Going through a non-drug personal growth program had opened a crack in his structure, and his psychedelic sessions have been a wedge to push him through to greater openness. He has used ibogaine, mushrooms, harmaline, LSD, and MDMA.

In his first solo experience, Dick broke down a lot of resistance and got in touch with a deepened sense of love for others. This has led him to no longer discriminate against people. He now realizes how important it is to have a support system. He has found that he is no longer interested in giving unsubstantiated opinions, but needs facts. Otherwise, communication is a waste of time. Before he loved picking holes in other people's positions, and considered himself a real "shit stirrer," which made people around him uncomfortable. He was a master of finding errors; one slip and they were dead. Since he is less preoccupied with himself, he can see others better, which has opened up relationships in many ways.

Dick's experiences in the psychedelic program have contributed to the cleaning up of specific areas of his life. In one experience, he wrote a letter to his deceased father and feels that his relation to his father is now complete. There is a break in his relationship to his mother—they cannot talk because of her attitude—but he has dropped the resentment from his side and has written her a letter of complete validation. He would be in instant ecstasy if she would call him. He has made it his intention to be back in a relationship with his mother in two months and to have an excellent relationship in six months. However, he is willing to have it the way that she wants it.

His relationship with his wife is now magnificent. Having experiences together has broken down the barriers between them and has allowed him to see his deep commitment to her. Communication has been opened up and he now gets tremendous support from her. They can work things out between them and let each other have their own being and their own space, which includes space for good fights. They can no longer get away with crap and find it easier to just tell the truth and act.

The most satisfying benefit has been to discover that "he is not bullshitting anymore." These experiences have snapped his resistances and have had a total effect on all of his reactions. He has had powerful experiences of himself and other people and now responds out of who he is. Discussing specific changes, in the area of awareness Dick feels that he is clearer, more willing, and more open. He is much more aware of other people and their names and is more willing to be supported by them.

He has also had profound experiences of God which have increased his sense of connectedness to others and all things. He has found God and lost his fear of death. Dick was always aware of nature, but in his first experiences he was able to notice just how aware he was. He always saw the detail, but now he sees God everywhere. He has become less destructive to the environment and has cut out using pesticides. Gardening and mowing the lawn are jobs that are a thrill to do. He makes time for them even when he is pressed.

In the religious area, he used to think that the Catholic Church was God, and had gone to seminary. He has found God and his connectedness to the rest of reality in his psychedelic experiences. He reported that during one ibogaine experience, he was scared shitless. He left it in God's hands and was willing to feel whatever emotions were coming up. He has symbolically died twice during experiences. The result was loss of all fear of death.

Since beginning the psychedelic sessions, he has gone to glass school and a communication workshop and has signed up for the Course in Miracles. He has made a commitment to run in next year's marathon. He had previously considered that running any distance was ridiculous and used to make fun of his wife for running. He now finds that when he gets tired running, he can pull energy in through the palms of his hands. It is almost like having a session.

Dick has always been energetic, but he now finds that he wastes less energy. He has eliminated fretting, finding it easier to start producing results rather than fret over problems. He is more willing to confront failure, which releases energy for positive action. He is better able to focus energy and has discovered how useful it is when working with other people to have them all sit down and focus their energy together. Otherwise there is a tendency to act from an unconscious place which dissipates energy and life and is not as satisfying. If things are left to fate, one remains unconscious.

He and his partners, who are also in the psychedelic program, now have more significant relations with their clients and feel that they make a difference in people's lives. They have endeavored to clear out all unconsciousness from their business operations, getting together to go over the operation and plan the work. They have hired a consultant, changed the name of the business, studied the market, and reviewed all aspects of the operation in order to carefully choose their direction. Finally, they have shifted the context of their business from profit-making to being a source for their favorite charity. This was scary at first, as it was hard to ask people for donations and risk losing their business.

With regard to creativity, Dick is now aware that he can be the creator. He is willing to let go of the past and has more facility producing new, different designs and having them be exactly what he wants. He can stay with an idea and keep working until it is just right. The improved focus on creative work has lead to an award-winning design. Clients are now ordering larger pieces, worth two to three thousand dollars.

Dick has had to learn how to get free of his own thoughts and the thoughts of others and address the person and the context. He has found that focusing on reality creates realities. He can change reality instantly by confronting the context and not what people think about it. This leads to very positive results and is freeing and ecstatic. This approach can be used anywhere to plough through the junk in life. In a personal growth program, he learned to understand the concept of coming from context rather than content, but he found that he had to experience it before he could use it. Now by owning the project, he can make it work.

Mentally, he has experienced the meaning of larger contexts, which has been freeing and ecstatic. Formerly, he was unable to imagine a context larger than himself. He can also experience the power of operating from a larger context.

Dick has testified that he finds it extremely important to plan his experience ahead of time and know what he wants. He feels it is very important to have psychedelic experiences together with those to whom you are close. In such cases, it is good to share with the others ahead of time what you wish to get out of the experience. Having a psychedelic experience is a tool to be used when it is necessary. It is not a good enough purpose to just go along: One must be clear upon entering, and use the experience as a tool. He is confident that what happens depends on the way that you enter and how willing you are to have it the way that you want. He has found that it is difficult to have it very, very good, and this is sometimes harder than dealing with a problem. He also found that if he didn't want problems during an experience, he didn't have to have them.

Detrimental effects occur mostly when he is coming down from experiences. He usually goes through a period of agitation when the chemical is wearing off. Also, he doesn't like to go to work the next day.

CAROL

Carol, 36 years old, started her professional career as a teacher, but dropped this to work in administration at a university. During her psychedelic program she decided to go to graduate school and study psychology. She had a job in research, followed by an internship in which she counseled people. She ultimately returned to working with children, where she could combine her training in both education and psychology. She is now in private practice, specializing in working with youngsters.

Carol started therapy with Jacob at age 23, participating in a Gestalt Therapy group. She had no previous experience with psychedelics. She was unhappy with herself and was impressed by what some of the other members of the group had to say about their psychedelic experiences. She admired and respected the other members of the group. From their commentaries, she thought a psychedelic experience might be a good tool for her to get in touch with herself. She has since had around 50 experiences over a period of 13 years, about one half of which were on her own with friends.

She has tried just about everything: LSD, ibogaine, mushrooms, MDA, MDMA, mescaline, peyote extract, TMA-2,[2] harmaline and ketamine. Her favorite material has been ibogaine, followed by MDMA. Beyond these, the choice depends on her mood. While psychedelics have opened her up, she feels that she has also benefited from other personal growth programs, meditation, and healthy eating.

One of Carol's most memorable experiences was a very heavy trip with harmaline during the time that she had been studying behaviorism in school. She imagined herself walking down a one-way street like a movie set, acting out behavior that wasn't appropriate. At the end of the one-way street was a bucket, and she would throw up in the bucket. As she experienced this in her mental imagery, she would actually throw up. The whole scene visually, kinesthetically, the whole situation of behavior would end up with her throwing up into the bucket. Then after a while, she would be on same street again doing a different behavior, feeling it all out and throwing up. A whole series of inappropriate behavior ended in her throwing up this way. This was a very strong lesson in her kinds of behavior, where they were getting her, and where the pain and suffering came from.

A bucket and a box of kleenex used to be important adjuncts to her psychedelic journeys, but not so much any more. Either she has cleaned out her stuff or found a different way of operating.

Carol has opened up to her own feelings and is better able to feel them, even though they may not necessarily be pleasant. During psychedelic journeys, feelings are sometimes unpleasant, even painful. In a supportive, encouraging situation, she is able to feel these difficult emotions and ultimately accept them, which makes her more sensitive to the feelings of others. She now knows that the emotional discomfort will pass and afterward she will feel more energetic, more connected, and there will always be some benefit. She finds real value in facing fear and believes there is no rational reason for fear. She feels the fear when confronting it, getting down to it. Then it comes to the surface. She no longer resists it but finds she is freed from it. Having been through the fear, she can move on.

Before this program, she didn't get along well with either parent or her older brother. Now she gets along well with all three. All the areas of growth activity, including graduate school, contributed to improving these relationships. Her psychedelic experiences had a strong influence on these changes.

Carol reports being more connected to nature. This derives both from psychedelics and meditation. She finds much similarity between the two. She often meditates when on psychedelic journeys, and has psychedelic-like experiences when meditating. Her fiance teaches insight meditation, where

---

[2] For a description of these compounds, see Shulgin, A. T. & A. Shulgin, *PIHKAL*, Berkeley.

one watches one's breathing and anything that comes up. This enhances awareness and introspection, leads to compassion, and helps gain insights into connections with the world. It is based on Buddhism. One notices how everything changes. Most days she spends an hour a day meditating. She has experienced a very intense three month meditation retreat with 100 people where there was no talking.

She has an improved ability to get her attention off of herself; this frees a lot of energy tied up in fruitless energy loops. She feels she has gotten past her mind and has cut through a lot of verbal dialogue and chatter. She has a deeper sense of what's going on. She finds herself more centered, more grounded.

Earlier in her life, Carol wanted to get married, and wondered if she ever would. Then came a period of not wanting to get married and thinking that she never would. This was followed by once more wanting to marry, and now she is getting married to a man with whom she shares psychedelic experiences. Psychedelic sessions definitely helped to sort things out, cut through arguments, and create the space to be open to communicate and hear what each other has to say.

Prior to meeting her fiance, her psychedelic experiences helped her to get clear on who she is and who she wants to be with, how she wants to act, and what kind of behavior is appropriate. Her relations with friends have improved considerably. Some of her best and closest friends are in the psychedelic group and they share their experiences. A number of times when there has been trouble, a shared journey clears up what's going on. It permits Carol to put herself in the other person's shoes and helps her become more compassionate. Two days later, she can often see the other person in a totally different space in the relationship. She doesn't necessarily need to talk about what the problem was. She feels this is a big area where psychedelics have helped her to relate more easily to people.

Carol feels she has become more forgiving and doesn't beat herself up as much. She hesitates on this point because before her psychedelic program she was politically more active. She wonders if she's become less ambitious or driven. However, she observes that before her activities were more like racing her motor; now she feels that what she is contributing is more rewarding and fulfilling. As a college student, she was in the streets, sitting in at gatherings. Her psychedelic experiences started after she finished college. Now she is much less politically active. She still volunteers at a local school six hours a week as community service. She now wants a greater sense of satisfaction from her volunteer work and prefers to be one-on-one rather than work in a large organization. She enjoyed being in an anti-nuclear march recently and contributes large sums of money to meditators which will be a retreat center, which she feels will be a positive contribution to the world.

Carol feels she has become aware of barriers, obstacles, and things that she does to sabotage her own energy. Her psychedelic experiences connect her more with what she really wants and where she's really going; she is more in touch with her priorities, and doesn't waste as much time. This is more fulfilling, and raises her energy level.

She noted several changes in her work attitude. Previously she was more afraid; she felt she had to do certain jobs or be fired and be out in the cold. Now she is more creative, competent, and not so self-pressured. Her career goal changed several times. She is now more accepting of change, and doesn't need a single lifetime goal. Goals drop or change; she is more fluid. These changes have covered some 20 years.

Carol finds herself more perceptive, feeling that she has less to guard against. She is more willing to see herself in others, less judgmental, "better able to see what's going on," and more compassionate. Since compassion leads to higher awareness, she doesn't have to struggle against what she sees. This makes her more accepting and aware. Sometimes this is painful if there is a time lag between becoming aware of something she is not happy with and accepting it. A consequence of these shifts in her awareness is that she feels more confident, more at ease and more trusting, which allows her to put more energy into doing than wondering how she'll do it.

Carol reports feeling a lot more alive. She thinks she looks younger. She feels younger, less dragged out, healthier, and more spontaneous. She feels that her intuition is much stronger. She trusts her intuition more and it has developed and grown. She has much more creativity, again because she trusts herself more, and is more relaxed when looking at situations.

Carol's quality of life has improved immensely. Before psychedelics, she had no sense of fulfillment. She is happy that this has reversed. She participates in more recreational activities, enjoys them more, and does more of what she likes to do. She is more efficient in doing what chores and housework need to be done to make life pleasurable and satisfying. She is more careful about diet and gains satisfaction from exercise. Psychedelic experiences are sometimes recreational, but this she can't count on.

Carol describes two effects that could be considered harmful. The first is that her memory is sometimes a little shaky. This might be due to a lot of marijuana smoking; she has also consumed a lot of alcohol. She sometimes wonders if there is any correlation between memory loss and taking psychedelics. She has cut back more on alcohol and marijuana than on psychedelics. The other adverse effect was that she recently got a bad kidney infection after an experience with MDMA. She probably picked this up when she was in Asia, but she felt that the MDMA experience may have lowered her resistance and permitted the kidney infection to manifest. She feels that in general, MDMA is not good for the body.

In conclusion, Carol was at first alienated from God or the spiritual. She felt unhappy and had psychological problems. She hoped she might be helped and was open to trying. Her psychedelic program was a long transition for her. She gradually let down and extended her boundaries. At first she felt tremendously isolated and alone. She had friends but was not really connected with other people. She no longer feels that she ends with her physical body, but is much more connected to the world; first with friends, then objects of nature, then more and more with the whole world. It is still hard for her to use the word God. It is not intrinsic to her vocabulary. She's a Buddhist and is very trusting of the process.

Carol feels the most important aspect in the use of psychedelics is the group context that she has experienced. The person leading the group, its structure and the attitude of the participants are more important than the use of the substances. It's about people not seeking quick thrills but earnestly searching for greater spiritual or personal growth.

SALLY

Sally is 29 years old and is married to Dick. She is a partner with him and another woman in a stained glass business. She also does some work in massage. She has been in the psychedelic therapy program with Jacob for about one year, and has had ten to twelve experiences over this time. The psychedelics she has used include LSD, ibogaine, mushrooms, and MDMA.

Sally discovered in her first experience that life is about expressing what she calls the Real Self, a concept which she had not previously explored. After her first trip alone, it was very evident to her that there was a Spirit, an entity higher than herself that was part of her. She has found the psychedelic sessions helped her to cut through the layers of unconsciousness that keep her from realizing her true nature. This newfound ability has allowed Sally to progress in her personal growth at a rate that she never before thought possible. Problems and situations arise rapidly and are quickly resolved.

Most of her life Sally had beat herself up, been unforgiving of her own limitations. After some very uncomfortable experiences, she has learned to no longer do that. On her first trip with MDMA, at 75 mg., she felt she was wrung completely out and that elephants ran all over her body. On this experience, she went through all of her fears. She meditated for five hours in the bath room; she had never felt so horrible in her whole life. It was terrible. She determined that she would never again put herself through such torture. Since then, she has had no physical discomfort when doing MDMA; perhaps, on occasion a little nausea.

Sally's relationships with other people have changed since she began her sessions with Jacob. Her relationship with her family has improved tremendously. She is now much closer to her family than she has ever been. This started with her very first experience. Everyone in the family has come to understand that even when problems do arise that it does not affect the feeling of love that they share for one another. This deepening of connectedness can be seen in Sally's relationship to her sister. She always got along fine with her sister, but they did not communicate with each other very often. The relationship was nonchalant. After starting the psychedelic program, she began to talk to her sister more often, and the relationship deepened. They still don't see other often, but they are now very loving.

She describes her marriage relationship now as magnificent. She and Dick have been married nine years. They are deeply committed to each other, and hold their intention to maintain the relationship even when they are fighting. Before beginning the program there were issues in the marriage that she could not acknowledge or break through. But the psychedelic experiences permitted breaking through them, even exploding through. An ibogaine experience that Sally and Dick shared particularly illustrates this point. This session blew the lid off of the relationship. It came to their attention they were not being truthful about a lot of things in their lives. They took a good look at their commitment to each other, and felt very committed despite their old issues that were resurfacing. They found it was very important to have the experience together, as it created a safe space for complete sharing and open, honest communication.

Sally's professional life has also seen improvement from her involvement in Jacob's psychedelic program. Sally, Dick, and their partner hired a business consultant and installed better management systems. They are committed to cleaning up unconsciousness in their operation and improving communication. The quality of their glass work and the panels they produce has substantially improved. She also notices a difference in the way she massages people. She used to work intently. Now she works more slowly and feels it is much more healing. She puts herself in the place of being God, just as in a psychedelic journey. She feels that by doing this it allows her to connect more fully with her clients and their particular needs. The change is wonderful. She feels that miracles really happen with people on the massage table. Sally now views her massage work as a means to communicate with the higher Self and to contribute to the healing of her clients, whereas before her psychedelic experiences, she was just working with people's muscles. Sally states that she now has more energy, a stronger ability to focus, and greater healing ability. She claims that there is no comparison between the way these things used to be and the way they are now. She is absolutely clear that she can heal—not by doing the healing but by being a conduit for healing.

With regard to chores like housekeeping, Sally feels that giving service is a fulfilling pursuit. It's a way of being responsible for life and being a source for relationship. Sally now sponsors two children in a ten day course for 80 youths at risk. These are kids who could go one way or another in their life. Her sponsorship is a lifelong commitment. This comes out of directly wanting to help keep their hope alive.

Concerning attitudes toward social issues, Sally had been exposed to the difference between content and context in EST (Earhart Seminar Training). However, this difference was not really comprehended until she started her psychedelic program, which has made it much easier to distinguish between the two. Now she can readily transcend chitchat into the bigger picture.

Sally once had doubts that she could create new life. In one of her sessions, she experienced life fully. She knows that life is about *now*, and that she is responsible for life. The feeling was like giving birth. Now she knows she can create new life. A crucial part of this experience was seeing Dick's mother, and realizing she could make life now. For Sally, part of choosing life is having children, and she knew that Dick's mom will live in her children. She was willing to make life right for her mother-in-law so that she can continue to live on in her grandchildren. Sally's willingness will help bring it about.

Sally has come to realize more fully the importance of continually participating in the world around her, to keep expanding her realm of experience. She has sought out more personal growth workshops and has sought to develop neglected parts of her life. One such development is that Sally has started singing again. She used to sing when she was quite young, but as she grew through puberty into adulthood her ability was covered up with uncertainty and fear, and she could no longer do it. On one of her journeys, she was very moved upon hearing a classical version of "Danny Boy." She discovered then that she really likes singing. She saw the whole universe laid out before her, and that she could do anything she wanted. When she asked what she should do, God replied, "Sing." She started taking singing lessons. Her husband reported that her voice has changed; it has expanded and opened up and has a much better sound quality. One interesting incident during an experience occurred when she was singing; she noticed that insects landed on her. When she stopped singing, they flew off. She has no explanation, but has good retention of the event.

Through her psychedelic experiences, Sally has become more of a spiritual person. After her first trip alone, it was very evident to her that there was a Spirit, an entity higher than herself and that was part of her. She finds that love is communication with God. Once Sally had accepted this notion into her life, she experienced an immense respect for everyone in her life.

Sally finds ibogaine has the most lasting effect of all the substances. It "really hangs in there," and it provides much material to evaluate and gain insight from. On her last ibogaine experience, it took her seven days to reenter her previous state of consciousness. She became quite shaky by days four and five, and was very upset. Then, all of a sudden, she was completely back into life again. Overall, it was an excellent experience in which she saw that everyone is connected to Spirit. This connection was illustrated during the session by the image of a flame. Now when she talks to people, she directly addresses the light or spark which resides within us all. Knowing this has allowed Sally to better understand and more effectively communicate in her dealings with people.

When asked if she has experienced any detrimental effects, Sally says that it often seems like she had difficulties when she was in the middle of a journey, or even a couple of days afterward. But when the experience is complete she always knows that it was very valuable. There have been no detrimental bodily effects.

Sally now knows that there's a Universal Mind out there. It never stops generating; it's an endless creating machine. One can learn to participate in the process.

APPENDIX II: TRIBUTES TO LEO ZEFF

SARAH ZEFF

A Daughter's Tribute—Spring 2003

I KNEW AS A YOUNGSTER that my father was involved in extraordinary and unique work. As I grew into my teens, he shared more of the specifics of the work and the need for keeping it quiet. He also offered me the opportunity to experience the world of hallucinogens whenever I felt I was ready.

At about the age of 18 he and I both decided the time had come for me to know, first-hand, the wonders of the psychedelic realm to which he was devoting much of his life. And so I was inaugurated into the inner sanctum of his world. I met and became friends with many of the people with whom he worked. They were all very committed to using these substances in thoughtful, therapeutic ways, yet most of them also delighted in the joy and fun the experiences offered. Leo increasingly surrounded himself with others who were dedicated to the work, people with whom he could share anecdotes and personal notes from their own trips or the trips of others.

As an adult, my life diverged from my father's, yet we remained close and he continued to share with me the work he was doing and the people he helped—the people whose hearts were so open after a trip that their worlds were forever altered in ways no talk therapy could ever have achieved. Here are some of the more remarkable stories I remember. (The names have been changed.)

One of the first stories he told me was that of Chandler, a 60-year old man whose body was riddled with cancer. In 1965, there was only a primitive kind of chemotherapy available, and after everything possible had been done, they sent him home to die. Being already part of Leo's "family," he was able to spend many weekends with the group he loved, tripping and opening his heart. In one of his post-diagnosis trips, he experienced his own death.

This is not an unusual phenomenon with hallucinogens, but for someone staring death in the face, it must have delivered a considerable emotional punch. In the aftermath, the group lovingly helped him go deeper into the experience by planning and carrying out his (mock) funeral.

The epilogue to the story of Chandler is that he didn't die of this cancer. The tumors disappeared. His is one of a handful of miraculous cancer turn-around stories that medical science cannot explain. At the time, the dumb-founded Chandler, his biological family, and Leo's family speculated that it had something to do with the psychedelics. It may have—or not—and he lived to enjoy many more years with a very open heart.

Somewhat less dramatic than Chandler, yet life-changing, was Benjamin. Ben was a homely, shy Jewish man in his late 40s when he began traditional talk therapy with Leo in the early 1950s. He had been born with a deformed leg, which gave him a nasty limp and an ongoing level of pain that was worsening as his muscles got older and stiffer. Ben was an elementary school teacher. He had no surviving family, a very poor self-image, never married, and his only sexual experiences had been with prostitutes. His students disliked him and ridiculed him behind his back, making his job very unpleasant. He was, in Leo's words, a miserable, joyless man.

By 1966, Ben had been in therapy with Leo for almost ten years, without so much as a modest breakthrough. For Ben, "Dr. Zeff" was someone he could talk to; not much else happened. As Leo gained confidence in the administration of the substances (then primarily LSD), he began to consider Ben for a trip. He talked to him about it and Ben, now in his 50s, agreed that it might be worth a try.

In his very first trip, Ben broke through years of misery, cried for the first time in differences, and shared a hug—also his first—with Leo. By the time I was inaugurated into "the family" and met Ben, he had been a member for many years. Although he was still in some pain and presented himself as a cautious, serious man, he was also quick with a hug and a smile. The group truly was his family, the only one he had ever known, and he joined them once a month to trip and to open his heart.

My father was passionate in his zeal for helping people overcome addiction. In the late 1960s, Leo and other practitioners began to discover that some of the substances held great hope as cures for addiction. That news traveled fast and Leo's friends and colleagues began a steady stream of referrals of alcoholics and drug addicts.

Some of the referrals could not pass Leo's rigorous screening and therefore could not participate in the work. But there were many who did pass and one of them was Peri. Peri had tried to kick her alcohol habit many times, but always returned to it when life got rough. Leo agreed to give Peri a trip. Through it she experienced feelings that she had previously deadened with liquor. Over time, with Leo's help, Peri took many trips and learned to accept those feelings, and with that acceptance came less reliance on alcohol. That pattern repeated itself over and over again, with alcoholics and people addicted to a wide spectrum of other drugs.

Chandler, Ben, and Peri were only three of the hundreds of amazing stories my father told me over the years—stories of ordinary people who made life-altering breakthroughs in their ability to lead happy, productive lives and relate more lovingly to the people who shared their world. There was never a doubt in my mind that he was doing good work. I have rarely known anyone who had as much passion for his work as he did. All he ever wanted from his life was the ability to help people lead happier lives. He enjoyed the occasional recognition that came his way in later years, but no accolade or honor ever meant as much to him as a single human being telling him how much his knowledge, wisdom, and willingness to do this work had changed their lives. He surely left the world—and me—richer for having known him.

HENRY ZEFF

A Son's Tribute—Fall 2003

AS I SIT TO WRITE THIS, I am looking at a photo of Leo with his full beard, at the height of his Guru stage. I don't know of any one else, personally, more qualified to wear the title of the Secret Chief. He was always a friend to anyone, at any hour of the day or night.

I remember many times, when I would be visiting overnight, the phone would ring with a late night call from a friend or a member of his extended family, in the middle of some personal problem, a bad trip, or whatever. Leo would answer, always with a soft voice no matter what the hour, and then with wisdom, humility, compassion, and Yiddish sayings. He was a master at work, rarely anxious, always patient and kind—to patients, friends, family and strangers alike.

My brother-in-law and his dad hadn't spoken a word in many years due to child/parent disagreements. Then at my sister-in-law's wedding, Leo spoke with the father for maybe a half hour and the father and son were able to converse as if they were old friends. The miracle at the wedding, I call it.

I don't know how many people's lives Leo touched like this and a thousand other ways throughout the years, in his profession as a psychologist, with and without the "materials" he used, and as a friend and caring person to all he knew.

His eagerness and excitement over each new material that became available was amazing. He was like a true scientist ever ready to check out another way to do the needed job.

His life was an amazing collection of experiences, from growing up dirt poor to finding a home in scouting and then the Army. To college and his degree in psychology, to the wild and crazy 60s, and then his version of a more peaceful, saner 60s. Then the 70's and the new materials of that age.

He was ever humble and quiet about his work and experimentation, even when he began to see the fruits of his work. He had to stay quiet; to be famous in his time was to cease to be able to help.

It is sweet to see Leo finally get some credit for the mark he made on the world of his time and the world to come as well. He truly was *a Secret Chief.*

"ANDREW"

Underground MDMA Guide trained by Leo

In the 1970s, I was living in California and was interested in personal, social, and spiritual paradigm change. So I asked somebody who was a role model for me in those regards, "Where can I have an experience with LSD?" She replied, "Oh, I thought you would never ask."

She introduced me to Leo. The protocol was not to volunteer information to people who might be interested. But if somebody asked and you sensed that the motivation was appropriate, you asked Leo for permission to share information in a more specific way. After recounting your personal experience to the person, they then might be introduced to Leo. I did a solo trip. LSD was the material during your introductory solo session. If you were a "good tripper" who could stay self-contained during your trip, then you might be invited to join the family. This meant that you could trip in a group of eight to twelve people on a weekend.

There were all kinds of people: doctors, lawyers, merchants, and marginal kinds such as a pornographer. But you had to have enough money to pay him, and you had to know somebody who was on this path to introduce you. You would pay a therapist's fee for the private introductory interview. You paid a couple hundred dollars for your initial trip, and the group trips cost less. Materials cost an additional ten to thirty dollars. Leo's model was to pay separately for the materials so people did not get greedy, thinking that more was better. People had to be told that after a certain dose they were going to get undesirable side effects rather than increased benefit. Some people needed to learn about that.

There were people in the family who had a harder time coming up with money. They participated on a work exchange basis. They did thorough housecleaning before the other participants arrived. The aesthetics of the setting were important to Leo. He thought if somebody opened their eyes during a bad trip and saw a lot of dust, that might not support the development of their soul as much as seeing flowers and a fresh candle.

Actually, Leo was not as visually oriented as me. When he was working in his disciple's house, there was a girlie calendar on the wall in the kitchen. I was the first person who said, "You know, this doesn't contribute to making me feel safe for tripping." We didn't talk about it at length, but he took it down.

There were a variety of materials that were available: mushrooms and mycelium, MDA, and ibogaine. We originally tripped at night because that is how indigenous people do it. For urban people, that was quite a hardship. We did not have much time before and after a weekend. So Leo developed this daytime format so you would have time to come back from your trip in a completely rested state. People then had increasingly positive experiences. Now, a positive experience by Leo's standards was not what you experienced on the day of the trip. Leo believed the value of the medicine was what happened to your quality of life during the period that followed.

He made MDMA available to the group after he had experienced enough of it with Sasha Shulgin. By then, they felt confident that it was reasonable to introduce it to people like ourselves who were willing to experiment. Leo said every time that we are all experimenters. He emphasized that we did not know everything about these medicines, and although he was telling us the best that he knew, in fact nobody knew everything about them. One of my earliest trips was a mushroom trip. While coming down from the trip in that family setting, I got the very clear message "Do this every three months. Keep coming back even if you do not remember why." So I actually did it every three months for about five years.

Leo's groups had a consistent format. We sat around on Friday night in a talking circle. One by one, everybody told what was going on in their lives. If they had tripped before, they described what had happened to them since their last trip. You heard about a dozen stories, different issues that people were dealing with in their lives. You came to the realization that the nature of being human is to feel these struggles, contradictions, curiosities, longings, and pleasures.

Leo would review the instructions and the agreements. You were not to repeat to anybody where, when, or with whom you had this experience. You were not to leave the room without explicit permission from the facilitators. You would not do anything harmful to yourself or anyone else. There was to be no sex with anybody else.

The final agreement was Leo saying, "If I should at any time during the trip tell you to do something that you are not doing, or to stop something that you are doing, you will." He would look the person in the eye, and each participant would have to say "yes". Then Leo used to say "That means that if I told you to jump out a window, you would." He did not want it to seem like it would have to be something that would be clearly in our best interests, because in our tripping state it might seem like something that was against our best interests. So if he said, "Go fly now," we would say "Yes" without question.

Many people reported afterwards that it occurred to them during their trip to do inappropriate things. Then they remembered that they agreed not to do harm, and that they had agreed to do whatever they were told by the leader. Therefore, they would remember this and censor themselves. That turned out to be part of the freedom, not a restriction.

Not every group leader warrants being given that degree of trust. This sort of agreement was very delicate and strong. Then Leo would say to the group "I want you to know that I have never had to call on that, I have never invoked it, but you still need to agree to it because it is one of the agreements." Participants knew beforehand that every time they came they had to reaffirm the same commitment to the agreements. So the beginners in the group and the repeaters all came on a common playing field.

Then Leo gave advice. "If you don't know what to do and your mind wanders, then listen to the music. If you go into heavy judgments against yourself, then listen to the music." He instructed us not to interfere with other people's trips. This was altered for groups on MDMA, because Adam (MDMA) facilitates communication and compassionate connection.

After a lot of people in the family had experienced Adam, some people wanted to use it with softer agreements. There was a smaller group that met about once a month, just to take Adam. The MDMA group was less tightly structured than the family trips. For example, MDMA can have such sensuous body awareness that people wanted to be freer to be in each other's faces with the relational part. Participants in MDMA groups would have to ask a facilitator in order to have contact with anybody else. The facilitator would then ask the other person to see if it was okay for both people to communicate at that time. So there was physical (without being overtly sexual) as well as verbal contact between people in the MDMA group.

Leo looked at his notebook while going through this procedure each time.

(Later I also used a notebook when I ran my groups.) The group could see they were in a carefully protected environment. This standardized routine enabled participants to be confident that they could go as deeply as possible into their trip, without having to keep part of their attention focused on their own safety or what was going on outside them.

There was also a small ritual to taking the medicine. We stood in a line waiting for Leo and his assistant to send us off, one by one, with a bon voyage hug. Leo gave good hugs. He was not in any hurry. He said he did not know how it worked, but people claimed they got something profound when he hugged them. He would say, "I've got plenty of it, so take all you need." It was an energy transmission, like recharging your battery. It was based on his confidence, his clarity, and his generosity. There was a humor about him. Yet at the same time he seemed like the group's father. He reminded me of my father, and he made us feel safe. At the end of your send-off hug, he said the same words year after year. He would say "Have a wonderful trip!" Then you took your medicine and you were on your own. You went to your place. You got your pad and your comforts ready. Some people were on ayahuasca, others mushrooms, others MDMA, or whatever.

When you started to come out of your trip in the afternoon, Leo served his homemade chopped chicken liver dish as the first food you would eat. He was an older Jewish man from an Eastern European background, and he thought chopped chicken liver was the healthiest thing for you. He came around like a waiter with a platter of liver offering it to everybody. With a shorter acting material, like MDMA, some people were back by mid-day. Other people were still flat on their back and not yet ready to eat by supper. We were told not to talk about our trip that day. Everybody shared dinner. Then we went to bed.

Sunday morning there was a ritualized circle. Participants took turns describing what had happened during their trip. We would describe what we felt and did, in the manner of recounting a dream. But it was not about interpreting, except so far as the interpretation of it was part of the trip itself. Each participant would witness this incredible array of individual experiences that had occurred in the same room. You might see common threads and identify with someone else. Or somebody might seem uniquely different from you. Someone might even say

"I cannot remember anything because I have amnesia for my trip." This was the range of the human condition.

People would often be less judgmental toward themselves when they heard other people's stories. Similarly, people might learn new possibilities by looking at the variety of other people's experiences. When there was a sharing of experiences, somebody might come back three months later and say "When so-and-so said such-and-such in that circle, I took that home with me as part of my trip." Then Leo would say "Well yes, you were still in a somewhat altered state, even though you felt primarily returned, and it was part of your trip then."

We spontaneously used each other's learning. Certain experiences can be potentiated in a group setting, even while you are having your own inner journey. This is separate from any psychic ideas about shared tripping and group consciousness. Leo always encouraged people to have their own individual trip, although I know that some other groups got together with the purpose of working on group projects.

During the period when I was tripping regularly, I had a profound sense of community even with people I had never met, knowing that all over the world there were others who also knew that everything is connected. Bonds were made as our group developed. People fell in love and got married. Leo would say, "You don't want to make any life-changing decisions until at least three weeks after the trip. You don't want to move. You don't want to quit a job and take another one. You don't want to leave a relationship and start a new one. Just be with it a while. See what pertains to the trip itself and what is meant to be actualized in your life." That always seemed like good advice.

When somebody entered the family, they were given a small chalice. The glass cup had relief designs of blooming flowers on the silver stem and base. In the early days, Leo gave these to somebody who did the solo trip. They were from Mexico, and later they were not available anymore. Then a flat rolled silver version was distributed. So if you ever saw one of these cups in someone's house, then you knew they were in the same family. It was a symbolic way of recognizing when you were in the home of a family member. I later ran a group that had a comparable thing we distributed. After five years in Leo's group, I brought in my partner. While he valued the experience he did not like that particular setting. We both had facilitator skills and immediately wanted to share this process. The first time we hosted a group MDMA trip was in 1980. My partner asked me what I wanted for my birthday. I replied that I wanted to take MDMA together with some intimate friends. We chose about six people who we were close with or wanted to be closer to. He made the arrangements. The group went well. We had already developed a workshop circuit doing other kinds of personal development activities over in Europe. Therefore, we had access to a network of Gestalt therapists. Although they were not particularly interested in MDMA, they connected us with psychologists who we trained in West Germany. After getting to know and trust a few German psychologists, we told them about this new thing called MDMA. We invited them to share this experience with us. Then they wanted to invite some of their friends the next time that they came.

Our MDMA groups were this beneficial contribution that just sort of happened without planning. We were doing this regularly, primarily in Germany, but also Austria, Switzerland, Holland, Hungary, and Czechoslovakia. We started gradually in 1981. By the next year it really got going. We really had quite a community. Many participants returned at three-month intervals. Some brought along people who were significant in their lives.

There are a lot of retreat centers in Europe. Sometimes the people who provided these sites knew about our work and participated. Other times they had no idea what we were doing. We sat for about twenty groups of twenty people per year. That was 400 trips a year. Two thirds of those people were repeaters who were coming back. This continued until we stopped this work in 1988.

Our weekend workshops were completely based on Leo's model. There were only two changes to his protocol. First, we used only MDMA. We lived in America, but frequently visited Europe, so we would not be there to provide care afterwards. Therefore, we only used MDMA because it has a low incidence of prolonged reactions. If you sit for thousands of sessions, you do see some rough experiences.

The other change was that we did not personally interview everybody before the trip. The new people got cleared by the person who had been there before. If there were any concerns about the appropriateness of the new individual, such as health problems, then we would say, "No, we cannot take the risk." About a dozen psychologists from different cities became interested in starting their own groups. They seemed sufficiently mature, so they informally apprenticed with us. Once MDMA became freely accessible, I heard of people working with it who I wished were not. Still, I still think the lack of official control was more good than bad.

After experiencing MDMA, one of our clients talked for the first time to her parents about their experiences during World War II. This is a very big issue in Germanic Europe, with that older generation dying out with this great silence about the war. Another of our German clients was the daughter of a Nazi officer. She spent a lot of her childhood locked in a closet because he was a sadist, or did not know how to properly raise children. She was born with normal vision, yet became completely colorblind after prolonged isolation in the closet. As an adult she worked as an artist without being able to see color. She came to trip with us many times when she was in her thirties. She tripped hard, which is unusual on MDMA. She would vomit. She was terrified. She would think about suicide. One time while she was tripping, she decided that she wanted to die because it was too difficult.

That was the only instance in my experience when the quality of the sitting was extremely important for the outcome. I did not tell her not to kill herself; I just really stayed with her. She sometimes had a sense of breakthrough. Memories from childhood would come back to her. She returned to trip again three times a year for a year or two. We would ask her why she kept coming back if it was so unpleasant. She replied that she felt that she was, millimeter by millimeter, making progress. At one point while tripping she said, "I can see color!" From then on, her color blindness was cured.

"KATHERINE"

I WOULD LIKE TO REPORT a great experience I enjoyed in 1970 at Leo's home. In those days, if you were very lucky indeed, you might have been invited to participate in what was called a "guided trip." The idea was that under supervised conditions, psychedelics could provide an experience that mystics might work for years to be able to have.

On arrival, my husband and I were asked to do "withholds," an exercise that was meant to dispel any negative "charge" that we might have toward each other. Then Leo gave us some guidelines: we were not to leave the house, for our safety. We were not to engage in sex—that wasn't what this was about. We were each to have our own experience, and not disturb the other. We were there to take a look at the contents of our own minds, perhaps in a new light.

Well, all this sounded interesting and only mildly alarming, since Leo was a well-known and trusted friend. We lay on mats with blankets in front of his fireplace on his soft brown carpeting, looking up at a lovely bronze chandelier supported by a ceiling of natural wood. The large windows in the room looked out on his gardens, mostly big white shasta daisies. A stereo played soft popular music. Leo gave me a capsule containing large doses of both LSD and mescaline.

In a few minutes, I felt myself relax and sigh, and it seemed the whole house sighed. The appearance of the room seemed to soften, and the chandelier took on the appearance of a glowing jewel. Tiny dust motes seemed to shine like diamonds in the air. I had never understood my early religious training; I just didn't understand what was meant by "God," and had no concept of what was holy at all. But now it seemed my surroundings had taken on new meaning, and shone with an inner light that seemed *self-evidently* sacred.

Later I seemed to pass through other gateways and worlds, some terrifying (I thought I was drowning in blood, and seemed to experience a friend's violent and terrible suicide)—and some oddly just disgusting: things appeared vulgar, sordid, and sort of plastic.

As I was struggling with this ugly world, Leo came over to me and he said simply "When you've come to the end of your rope, just let go."

I didn't just let go. I threw that rope from me, and *leaped,* I knew not to what!

Instantly I was transported into a state of utter bliss. I seemed to be able to look at this silly creature that was myself - forever setting traps for myself, stepping into them, and then actually being surprised! From my delightful distance, all this seemed hilarious in the extreme, and I laughed with real delight until Leo began to look at me anxiously again. He looked, with his gentle brown eyes, like a worried seal, and I laughed some more. Then I worried I might have hurt his feelings and stopped.

I went back to enjoying my surroundings. Jacob had put on some music that related to my Christian upbringing, and I enjoyed the hymns with some nostalgia. I amused myself by creating pretty visual effects and then changing them. I think at this point I was returning to "normal." After a time I realized I was "back," with considerable regret; I did not ever want to leave that joyful place.

Leo kindly helped us to shower, and we slept comfortably.

I believe that I had a truly religious experience. For the first time I understood the nature of Heaven - being freed from my miserable self at last. Christ had said not to look for Heaven because it is all around us if we could only see it. Now I know what he meant - I've been there.

I think in psychedelic circles this is known as the experience of ego death. How odd that we should cling to something that is only a source of Misery.

Love to Leo!
A grateful student and friend

P.S. While I can't really judge how much this experience changed my life, I'm sure I'm much happier for it.

"RACHEL"

LEO, HIS WIFE, AND HIS CHILDREN were friends of my husband's mother from the synagogue up in Berkeley. My husband is the one who turned Leo onto marijuana. It was around May 1 of 1965 when we went to Leo's home, joined a group of other people, and had a group experience for the first time. My husband and I were the youngest people there. He was 30 and I was 25. It was a very interesting experience. I realized right away that most of the people were there to "get well" and there were some people with some severe problems. I did not have any that I knew about. I wanted to experience what was going on, and I did. One of the most interesting things that happened that night was we were all laid out in front of the fireplace downstairs and we had our earphones on and our eye shades on and then all of a sudden my husband sat up and called for Leo to come over. He said, "There is a woman upstairs way in the back. She's in trouble." Leo did not doubt him at all. He just went upstairs right where he said and that is where the woman was. She was in trouble. So we realized the power of what was going on. This was a powerful thing that we knew about but we had never experienced close up like that. That is how we met this woman, with whom we have been friends ever since.

There were things we wanted to know and that we wanted to experience. We felt we were perfect the way we were which included the potential for change. So perfection is where we were coming from. We did not have it that we needed fixing. We had it that there were things we did not know—things we had not experienced that we wanted to. When I first came into this program, I had some doubt as to whether there was some getting well to do or not. As I experienced more of these trips, I realized that there was not. Then I came to the realization that there was more to do, more to experience, more to have, more to give. It was just more, and at the same time, there is only what there is right now. It is a funny juxtaposition. My favorite medicine with out question was *yage* (ayahuasca). *Yage* and acid. That was my idea of a good time. It was a primitive sort of beast. You talk about dancing and the music becoming energy in your body—that is *yage*.

I remember seeing power, tribal, witchcraft sort of things on that drug specifically. One time I was a lion and I looked down and saw this lion's paw. It was huge, I just felt the power of that lion in my paw, and I just knew how strong a lion was. It is primitive, quite basic, and primal. My husband and I used psychedelics as a way to experience more sensuality. I was able to feel a lot more pleasure from the use of psychedelics. It became a rule in Leo's work that there would be no sex taking place. I respected Leo for putting together a situation where you could have a large group of people on the medicine in a safe way. By having a set, setting, and structure that people adhered to, it made it safe. I had an experience on mescaline and I remember that was all he had. I worried my way through half of the trip that I was going to waste the trip but then I settled down and I got with it. Then this music came floating through the air. I could see the notes and the clefs and then it just came. I was really going with it, then it started to go toward my crotch, and it turned into this snake. I snapped my legs shut, sat up and resisted it, which turned my life to shit. I just had the experience of resisting pleasure as not being a good thing and then I got back into my trip. I tried to get the snake back to make friends with the snake. Then the snake turned into an octopus. It was beckoning me. It took me down into the water and wanted me to come in a cave. I was scared but I went with it. He just wanted to show me where he lived.

I also used LSD in the groups to break through my sensuality barriers, whatever they were, to have more sensuality. I have spirituality tied up with sensuality. We met in that realm. I always believed in God. I always had this secret kind of pleasure knowing that Leo was Jewish too. I felt that it was a very highly spiritual experience. All of it. I did not think you had to be sick to have spirituality. Many of those people did. One of the goals of the group was explained to us this way. America is a new country. It was only a couple of hundred years old and we have come a long way as a country. He and other people wanted to know if psychedelics would enable people to deal with rapidly changing realities. Could problems be solved quicker or more efficiently? There were people in mathematics and architects brainstorming. There were tests going on about people who were stuck in places in their careers. Mathematicians, architects, chemists, artists, writers, and people who were stuck were given huge doses of mescaline and many of them just broke right through. So there were all kinds of things like that going on.

Maybe this could be used for our country to go on in an efficient manner. Up until a few years ago, my husband and I would refer to Leo jokingly as the guy who ruined our lives. We were kidding. He had a lot to do with our lives. I would be a different person if I had not experienced what he had to offer I feel blessed.

"JULIA"

FOR MY FIRST EXPERIENCE, Leo had set the stage in his office. He changed that office into a bank of flowers with every symbol you could think of in there—the crucifix, the Star of David, the Hindu symbols, everywhere you looked there were symbols but mostly there were living, beautiful flowers all around. When I took the medicine, I lay back in this ordinary spot which he had made very comfortable for me with a little foam rubber mat and the ceiling was phony squares of insulation and they began to sparkle. Then I began to dissolve, then I'd come back around again. I died 10,000 times. At some point the dying stopped and I was in a neighborhood. I was in a place that was highly manicured and ordered. Nothing was happening. The lawns were cut, the shrubs were trimmed, the houses were perfect. There were little iron fences outside the windows. Nothing. It was dead as a doornail. I was trying to get out of that area because I did not like it. At that moment Leo lifted up the eye mask and said, "Where are you now?" Now in reality he could have been doing his office work and his bills at his desk there while I was going off some place, but he did check in and I said, 'I'm stuck in the Midwest someplace and I can't get out." He said, "That's the way it should be. You should be there. Do not try to get out. Be there. Be there with it. Don't try to get out." At that moment the music changed from his usual warhorse scene which was romantic—Tchaikovsky to Handel's water music—and the conjunction of what he said and the music may have made a difference. I found myself on a hill overlooking a sparkling harbor and a city beneath it. I was dressed in tails and a top hat. I took my hat off of my head and made a big gesture over my head with my hand and lifted it off. Out of the hat came the most beautiful spray of stars you would believe. I laughed, and laughed. It was the beginning of change for me from being terribly depressed to another option.

I once overheard him say, "I became so sick of these people coming in with their depressions and their problems and offering other options and they're not being able to take any of them. I became so tired of that." Leo said he wouldn't say this until we were well into him and knowing the process.

In my group, people did seem to take other options. Most of them made significant changes. They were professional people. They didn't change really. When you meet them on the street you wouldn't see any changes, but in their lives they made different choices. When I was with Leo, I was involved with a guy that I was bored with but he was good to me. My experience changed everything. I just couldn't take the boredom anymore. I still keep in touch with some of them. They are like family. You know when you go home for Thanksgiving you've got those aunts and uncles. You know how they don't really fit in your life but they're there. That's family.

At that time we were not the only people that were experimenting with this kind of thing. There were a lot of people out there experimenting and we all had this kind of bond. There was something beyond that was momentarily apparent and it led to a huge openness.

Leo made a difference in those people's lives—a big difference. Sure made a difference in mine, but it's interesting to be asked now because it's so integrated that it's hard to separate it and it's been so long... Leo was such a leader. He had that military experience but he'd also had the experience of being a psychologist, being a Jew, being a Buddhist and being who he was and that combination made him such a fabulous leader. He provided some very strenuous structures on some people.

There was one woman who just could not stop talking. She'd engage you and then you'd be engaged and slowly you'd recognize that this thing was to go on for the next half hour. She was going to be right there in your face talking. It was never loud but terribly engaging and he saw it. He stayed with it for a couple of trips and then he finally said, "On this trip you are not allowed to talk at all." She was mad at him but she made some fabulous changes. She went from cosmetics to opening a massage school in San Francisco and became internationally known. She traveled all over the world with this business. My experiences with Leo affected my relationship with my own family as well. I would never have reunited with them in the same way. Leo started us off with pictures of ourselves before we ever took the medicine. In doing so, I had to write my mother and ask her for the pictures, and she sent me a whole suitcase full of these things from infancy all the way up to being a teenager. It gave me a window into her eyes and I saw my father holding me in a proud way. I've had a lot of differences with my father. They didn't end but it opened a door to beginnings.

"LAURA"

MY EXPERIENCE WITH LEO and his group intertwined with events that were part of the historical era itself and with other group experiences I had. I dropped LSD once before I met Leo and certainly would have found some other way to experiment with hallucinogens if I had not met him, as I was living on the cusp of the New York beatnik and California hippie worlds when I arrived in the San Francisco Bay area in 1965.

Leo's unique contribution to my life was his creation of a group within which it was possible to get agreement on what I experienced on hallucinogens. For this I am eternally grateful.

I first saw Leo after my first acid trip. I had arranged for a friend to "sit" with me. The trip started very well—I had read books about the psychedelic experience in preparation for my first trip, and my trip followed the experience as described in The Tibetan Book of the Dead by Leary, Alpert, and Metzner. However, my friend was not prepared to allow me the time and space to examine my own experience inwardly, and the end of the trip felt uncomfortable for us both. My friend referred me to Leo, and talking to him helped me to integrate the experiences of that first trip.

Leo's group trips added to the reality that seeing Leo alone had given me. The group setting nurtured a scientific approach to examining inner human experiences. The group gave me many opportunities to observe the experiences of others from the sidelines as well as through more intimate interactions. The group also gave me opportunities to have others tell me their observations of my trips, and provided opportunities to safely explore "hallucinations." For example, I saw a snake on a mat, knew intellectually that there was no snake, but had to get up and touch the spot that appeared to be a snake in order to have the "hallucination" end.

Leo's record-keeping gave me the opportunity to make scientific observations of the effects of different chemicals on perception and consciousness. We explored different doses, different substances and combinations of substances, taking "boosters" at various times during a trip, and, also using non-psychedelics such as Valium, Ritalin, and marijuana. I got to be expert enough to identify the type and combination of substances taken by observing my own experience and the behavior of others.

Beyond the "scientific" aspects, I experienced personal gratification in the areas of spirituality and musical awareness. I loved using earphones and appreciated the wide variety of music we listened to. In my profession at that time, social work, I became more attuned to the internal experiences of other people. Also, the weekends were just plain fun!

What is the aftermath of my experiences with Leo? For almost 40 years I, along with two friends I met at the group, have lived as part of a community. Within this last year one of my two friends died. I am at peace with death. This peace comes from having the reality of my own perfection and of the perfection of the universe I've created.

APPENDIX III: RESOURCES

THE BOOKS, WEBSITES, AND PUBLICATIONS on the following pages are recommended for more information about psychedelic therapy and related topics. This list serves as an introduction and is by no means all-inclusive.

Evaluating the Scientific Literature

Like the Secret Chief, many therapists in the United States have surreptitiously employed psychedelic substances in spite of their illegality. Once they discovered the efficacy of such substances, they could not in good conscience withhold such effective means of treatment from their clients despite the risk of incarceration. One of the unfortunate consequences of this situation is that experiences and results cannot be publicly shared, which deprives current practitioners of a great deal of valuable information.

Nevertheless, there are many publications which present promising work with psychedelics, including dramatic help for tough cases that had been impervious to conventional forms of treatment. The MAPS Psychedelic Bibliography, available at maps.org/resources/psychedelic-bibliography, compiles a number of other bibliographies of psychedelic research and includes thousands of references, some with full text PDFs. These include the MAPS MDMA Literature Review Project (which includes full text PDFs of most papers), the Hofmann Collection (with over 4,000 psychedelic research papers from the late 1940s to the early 1970s, most with PDFs), and a number of other bibliographies. Other compilations are cited at the end of this section.

A major problem is to know how to evaluate the various references. Much of the current public misunderstanding is the result of the position of mainstream professionals and government agencies who have concentrated on emphasizing only the negative aspects of psychedelic use, screening out any data that would imply usefulness. Dr. Roger Walsh[2] comments on the selective bias of public information:

- Barriers to research and publication appear to have resulted in a bias toward selective dissemination of predominantly negative information about the effects of psychedelics...

- There have probably been few areas in psychology that have been subject to as much misinformation and sensationalistic reporting by the media as psychedelic experiences. While preliminary clinical research suggested that they might have considerable research and clinical potential, the popular press preoccupied itself almost entirely with sensationalistic accounts of dangers. This media treatment soon resulted in the cessation of almost all research and a bias at many levels of society toward the dissemination of only negative reports...

- What seemed to be widely unrecognized was that large numbers of people appeared to have derived, at least from their own point of view, significant benefits from psychedelics, a situation markedly at variance with media accounts of their devastating effects.

In this same paper, Walsh describes submitting a paper to a reputable professional journal that included evidence suggesting that in some cases, people might find psychedelics beneficial. Surprisingly, the editor responded that the paper could be accepted only if any reference to positive effects of psychedelics was removed. Since this was a fairly open-minded editor, Walsh wonders at the chance of publication of positive statements in other places.

To clarify the various positions held, it may be helpful to refer to recent writing which sheds light on the conflicting perceptions of those who claim to be experts. The problem is that mainstream science holds a very limited view of the nature of the human being. Clarification of this situation is now being presented in the relatively new field of Transpersonal Psychology, which recognizes those aspects of human experience in which the sense of identity of self extends beyond the individual or personal to encompass wider aspects of humankind—life, psyche, and cosmos—validating the spiritual foundation of life. An overview of many of the aspects of transpersonal psychology is presented in the book *Paths Beyond Ego: The Transpersonal Vision,*[3] a compilation of articles by over thirty contributors knowledgeable in this field.

An extraordinarily comprehensive overview of all aspects of human development is presented by Ken Wilber in *Sex, Ecology, Spirituality: The Spirit of Evolution*[4] and in more readable form in *A Brief History of Everything.*[5] To again quote Walsh, a leading authority in the field of Transpersonal Psychology:[6]

- The aim of these two books is to trace evolution—physical, biological, and human—and to set it within the context of the perennial philosophy: the common core of wisdom at the heart of the great religious traditions. Human evolution—of brain and mind, society and culture—is traced from early hominids to today and related to phenomena such as the evolution of gender relationships, human relationship to the earth, technology, philosophy, religion, and more.
- The scope of the work is extraordinary. Only a handful of thinkers, such as Aurobindo in the East and Hegel in the West, have assembled such evolutionary visions. Yet Wilber's view is unique in not only providing a far-reaching vision, but also grounding that vision in contemporary research in fields such as cosmology, biology, anthropology, sociology, psychology, philosophy, and ecology.
- The crux of the most serious disagreements among psychedelic investigators is the value placed on objective experience versus subjective experience. Mainstream science, through the dictum "if it can't be measured, it's not science," by and large ignores subjective or interior experience in favor of the objective outside world. This leaves them living in, according to Wilber,[5] a "monological" world, or "flatland." In such a world, much of that which is of great value to humans is non-existent, such as the very essence of consciousness and the nature of the human mind. It is precisely these latter elements that are so effectively revealed through appropriate use of psychedelics. It is worth

reading *A Brief History of Everything* to observe how all aspects of humanity and life can be put into perspective, a perspective developed by a brilliant mind that has carefully examined the data from many areas of scientific research, as well as the world's spiritual disciplines.

Notes

Passie, Torsten. 1997. *Psycholytic and Psychedelic Therapy Research 1931-1995: A Complete International Bibliography.* Hannover: Laurentius Publishers.

Walsh, Roger. 1982. "Psychedelics and Psychological Well-being."

Journal of Humanistic Psychology. Vol. 22 No. 3, pp. 22-32.

Walsh, Roger, and Vaughan, Frances, eds. 1993. *Paths Beyond Ego: The Transpersonal Vision.* Los Angeles: Jeremy P. Tarcher/Perigee Books.

Wilber, Ken. 1995. *Sex, Ecology, Spirituality: The Spirit of Evolution.* Boston: Shambhala.

Wilber, Ken. 1996. *A Brief History of Everything.* Boston: Shambhala.

Walsh, Roger. 1996. "Developmental and Evolutionary Synthesis in the Recent Writings of Ken Wilber." *Revision.* Vol. 18, No. 4, p. 9.

Grinspoon, Lester, and Bakalar, James B. 1979. *Psychedelic Drugs Reconsidered.* New York: Basic Books, Inc.

Books

50 Years of LSD: State of the Art and Perspectives on Hallucinogens. A. Pletsher (Ed.). Parthenon Publishing; 1994. A series of papers on the historical, pharmacological, psycho-pathological, transcultural and clinical aspects of LSD, presented at a conference sponsored by the Swiss Academy of Medical Sciences on the 50th anniversary of the discovery of LSD.

Dark Night, Early Dawn: Steps to a Deep Ecology of Mind. Christopher M. Bache. State University of New York Press; 2000. "With moving honesty and rare lack of inflation, Bache has brought forth a conception of the human psyche that intimately reconnects the personal ordeals and awakenings of the individual to the larger collective suffering and spiritual transformation of the entire human species, at the most crucial of historical thresholds. This is a book to read soon and to integrate carefully."— Richard Tamas, author of *The Passion of the Western Mind: Understanding the Ideas that have Shaped our World View.*

The Discovery of Love: A Psychedelic Experience with LSD- 25. Malden Grange Bishop. Dodd, Mead & Company; 1963. This book is a detailed and fascinating account of a person's initial encounter with LSD. It also reveals the incredible power of a well planned and well-executed psychedelic journey. Beginning in 1961, and stretching over the next three years, the International Foundation for Advanced Study in Menlo Park, California, conducted research with LSD and mescaline, processing some 350 participants. As a historical record, Bishop's book provides an important firsthand account of these experiments from a participant's point of view. To follow a conservative, 54-year-old businessman's transformation into a person who values love above all else in life is a profound testimony to the power of this sacred medicine we call LSD.

The Doors of Perception I Heaven and Hell. Aldous Huxley. Harper Collins; 1954/1956. A demonstration of what a refined, prepared mind can do with the opportunity afforded by a psychedelic in observing nature, art, colors, and forms in their full glory, with a profound appreciation of the transpersonal and numinous aspects of life. These books more than any other in their time period encouraged many to investigate the psychedelic experience.

Drawing it Out: Befriending the Unconscious. Sherana Harriette Frances. Introduction by Stanislav Grof, M.D. Prologue and Afterword by Tanya Wilkinson, Ph.D. MAPS; 2001. "I do not know of any single document illustrating the extraordinary healing and transformative potential of psychedelics in a way that matches in its importance this book by Harriette Frances and the

unique illustrations that accompany it. Her ability to find artistic expression for the images and depth of her psyche is truly extraordinary!"
- Stanislav Grof, M.D., author of *LSD Psychotherapy.*

Drugs, Set and Setting: The Basis for Controlled Intoxicant Use. Norman Zinberg. Yale University Press; 1984. A pioneering book that illuminated the factors that permit some people to use illegal drugs, including psychedelics, in a controlled fashion.

Ecstasy: The Complete Guide. A Comprehensive look at the Risks and Benefits of MDMA. Julie Holland, M.D. (Ed.). With contributions from Andrew Weil, Ralph Metzner, Rick Doblin, Douglas Rushkoff, Sasha and Ann Shulgin, Rabbi Zalman Schachter, and others. Park Street Press; 2001. "MDMA is a unique compound with great potential for positive use. This is the most complete book about it, with much information to help people realize that potential as well as reduce any possible harm."– Andrew Weil, M.D., author of *8 Weeks to Optimum Health* and *Spontaneous Healing.*

Ecstasy: The MDMA Story. Bruce Eisner. Ronin Publishing; 1994 (second edition). A widely read summary of the history, usage and effects of MDMA.

Entheogens and the Future of Religion. Robert Forte (Ed.). Council on Spiritual Practices; 1997. "Entheogen" is the currently designated name for a psychedelic used for spiritual realization. According to Jonathan Ott, the word is derived from Greek and means "realizing the divine within. " Dr. Huston Smith says, "collectively, these essays constitute the best single inquiry into the religious significance of chemically occasioned mystical experiences that has yet appeared."

Exploring Inner Space: Personal Experiences Under LSD-25. Jane Dunlap. Victor Gollancz Ltd.; 1961. Written by a well known scientific authority whose books were so popular the publisher refused to let her use her correct name. Jane Dunlop describes in detail five outstanding experiences under the influence of LSD. More beautifully written and profound descriptions of remarkable LSD experiences probably don't exist.

Gateway to Inner Space: Sacred Plants, Mysticism and Psycho-therapy. Christian Ratsch (Ed.). Prism/Avery Publishing; 1989. A collection of essays by many leading researchers in the field of altered states of consciousness. Issues addressed include the medical use of psychedelics, "molecular mysticism," death and rebirth themes in shamanism, comparisons between meditative and psychedelic experiences, and states of tryptamine consciousness.

Hallucinogens: A Reader. Charles S. Grob (Ed.). Penguin Putnam, Inc.; 2002. A collection of essays by and interview with: Lawrence Bush, Gary Fisher, Albert Hofmann, Terence McKenna, Ralph Metzner, Jeremy Narby, Thomas Riedlinger, Glenn Shepard, Huston Smith, Myron Stolaroff, Rick Strassman,

Donald Topping, Roger Walsh, and Andrew Weil. A great deal of the misunderstanding regarding the nature of psychedelic substances arises from the fact that the majority of scientists and researchers who have examined these substances in the past have not understood the essential spiritual nature of mankind. This collection of authors are thoroughly familiar with the true potential of psychedelic substances due to their direct personal experiences with them. This is the only way these substances can be properly understood and appreciated. Dr. Grob has assembled a well-informed collection of writings on the nature of psychedelics.

*Handbook for the Therapeutic use of Lysergic Acid Diethyla*mide-25, Individual and Group Therapy. D.B. Blewett, Ph.D. and N. Chwelos, M.D. 1959. Despite being prepared in the late 1950s, this handbook contains some of the most informed and valuable data available concerning the effective methods of conducting LSD therapy. Available on the www.maps.org website.

The Healing journey: New Approaches to Consciousness. Claudio Naranjo. Pantheon Books. Random House; 1973. Incisive case reports about the therapeutic use of MMDA, MDA, ibogaine and ha rmaline. A classic in the field of psychedelic psychotherapy.

Higher Wisdom. Charles S. Grob and Roger Walsh (Eds.). SUNY Press; 2004 (in press). Eminent thinkers reflect on the continuing impact of psychedelics. Contains interviews with Betty Eisner, Ram Dass, James Fadiman, Gary Fisher, Peter T. Furst, Stanislav Gro f, Micheal Harner, Albert Hofmann, Laura Huxley, Zalman Schachter, Alexander T. Shulgin, Ann Shulgin, Huston Smith, and Myron Stolaroff.

The Human Encounter with Death. Stanislav Grof, M.D. and Joan Halifax, Ph.D. E.P. Dutton; 1977. A remarkable portrait of the experiment in which patients dying of cancer at the Maryland Psychiatric Research Center in Baltimore, Maryland were treated with psychedelic therapy.

The Ibogaine Story: Report on the Staten Island Project. Paul de Rienzo, Dana Beal & Members of the Project. Autonomedia; 1997. An account of the discovery and development of ibogaine as treatment for drug addiction, with a special focus on the political aspects of ibogaine research.

In Search of the Ultimate High: Spiritual Experiences through Psychoactives. Nicholas Saunders, Anja Saunders, and Michelle Pauli. Rider (an imprint of Ebury Press, Random House); 2000. An analysis of the cross-cultural and spiritual implications of altered consciousness produced by psychedelics. Featuring a fascinating collection of the accounts and insights that hundreds of truth seekers around the world have obtained from their thoughtful and reflective use of psychoactives. An excellent book for people who want to know more about the spiritual uses of psychedelics in contemporary society.

Insight Outlook. Albert Hofmann. Humanics New Age; 1989. A personal review of Dr. Hofmann's world view. He describes the early childhood mystical experiences that established his basic understanding. It was his desire to more completely understand the mystery of matter and the miracle of the plant world that led him to chemistry. He chose to work at Sandoz because their chemical explorations involved plant materials, thus leading him more directly to the understanding of nature. The book sets forth the major tenets of his philosophy, which was reinforced by the openings provided by appropriate use of LSD.

Ketamine: Dreams and Realities. Karl Jansen, M.D., Ph.D. MAPS; 2001. "Indispensable reading for those with any interest in ketamine. Entertaining, thought -provoking, and thorough."— Rick Strassman, M.D., author of *DMT: The Spirit Molecule.*

LSD, My Problem Child: Reflections on Sacred Drugs, Mysticism, and Science. Albert Hofmann. J.P. Tarcher, Inc.; 1983. This book traces how LSD originated, the discovery of its psychic effects, its applications to therapy, and the crushing developments that ensued from the widespread use of LSD as an inebriant. The book describes a number of valuable individual experiences, as well as visits with key figures like Aldous Huxley, Timothy Leary, and others.

LSD Psychotherapy: Exploring the Frontiers of the Hidden Mind. Stanislav Grof, M.D. Introduction by Andrew Weil, M.D. MAPS; 2001. Considered the most complete book on psychedelic therapy, this is a treasure house of all aspects of the work: history, procedures, client preparation, qualifications of the therapist, and more.

Pharmacotheon: Entheogenic drugs, their plant sources and history. Jonathan Ott. Natural Products; 1996 (second edition). The introductory Proemium is a must read for those wishing to understand the current political, social, and scientific dilemmas of psychedelic drugs.

PIHKAL: A Chemical Love Story. Alexander T. Shulgin and Ann Shulgin. Transform Press; 1991. Comprehensive, definitive guide to the psychedelic phenethylamines, such as mescaline and MDMA, and a great love story. Two parts: first the human story of the search for active mind compounds within a marriage of two active minds. Next, detailed catalog of the chemistry, characteristics of action and synthesis of 179 compounds and results of human assay at varying dosages.

Psychedelic Drugs Reconsidered. Lester Grinspoon and James

B. Bakalar. The Lindesmith Center; 1997 (third edition). Two of the world's leading experts on drug use provide the general reader with a comprehensive survey of psychedelic drugs and the scientific and intellectual issues they raise. The authors review the chemistry of psychedelics, their effects, and the history of human experience with them as well as assessing the potential value of the drugs. Excellent bibliography.

Psychedelics Encyclopedia. Peter Stafford. Ronin Publishing; 1992 (third edition). Highly readable book on history, background, preparation, chemistry, methods of use, results, and social implications of the known psychedelic drugs.

The Psychedelic Reader: Classic Selections from the Psychedelic Review. Timothy Leary, Ralph Metzner & Gunther M. Weil (Eds.). Citadel Press; 1993. Selections about the therapeutic, religious and legal aspects of psychedelic drugs from the first four issues of the Psychedelic Review (1963-1964), the journal edited by the Harvard psychedelic research team.

Psychoactive Sacramentals: Essays on Entheogens and Religion. Thomas B. Roberts (Ed.). Council on Spiritual Practices; 2001. In 1995, the Chicago Theological Seminary, along with the Council on Spiritual Practices, held a conference to examine the potential benefits and concerns related to employing entheogens in spiritual practice. Speakers included leaders in religion, mental health, research, and allied fields. The views of the participants have now been published in this book, which is a valuable collection of information in an exciting field.

Pursuit of Ecstasy: The MDMA Experience. Jerome Beck, Ph.D. and Marsha Rosenbaum, Ph.D. SUNY Press; 1994. Expanding on a study sponsored by the National Institute on Drug Abuse, the authors present a thorough and trustworthy review of the emergence and spread of MDMA use, the path toward illegalization, the diverse social worlds and scenes evolved around the use of MDMA and how they result in different experiences, why people use MDMA and what if anything makes them stop, long term benefits and therapeutic potential, adverse reactions and abuse, and recommendations for harm reduction and continuing research of the therapeutic potential.

Realms of the Human Unconscious: Observations from LSD Research. Stanislav Grof, M.D. E.P. Dutton; 1976. A systematic and comprehensive discussion of the transpersonal model of the human unconscious. A uniquely valuable contribution to the field of psychology.

The Road to Eleusis: Unveiling the Secret of the Mysteries. R. Gordon Wasson, Carl A. Ruck, Albert Hofmann. Harvest/ HBJ; 1978. Three scholar-scientists document their theory of the LSD-like component of the religious rites at Eleusis, celebrated for 2,000 years.

Shivitti: A Vision. KaTzetnik 135633. Gateways Books; 1998. An autobiographical account of a concentration camp survivor's experiences with LSD psychotherapy, conducted in Holland by Professor Bastiaans. Very moving and illustrative of the processes of LSD psychotherapy.

Storming Heaven: LSD and the American Dream. Jay Stevens. Harper Collins; 1987. A thorough, well written, intensively researched history of the advent of psychedelics on the American scene. With each new aspect introduced, the author traces back to the roots of that development, and shows how it progresses to intertwine with the overall picture.

Thanatos to Eros: Thirty-five Years of Psychedelic Exploration. Myron J. Stolaroff. VW B-Verlag for Wissenschaft und Bildung; 1994 (see page 172 for complete description).

This Timeless Moment. Laura Huxley. Mercury House; 1991. A personal account of Aldous Huxley's last years by Laura, his wife, including details of the outcome of his request to be administered LSD while dying. Profoundly inspirational.

TIHKAL: The Continuation. Alexander T. Shulgin and Ann Shulgin. Transform Press; 1997. A continuation of the Shulgin's popular book *PIHKAL: A Chemical Love Story.* The first part of the book blends travel, botanical facts, scientific speculation, psychological and political commentary. The second part describes in detail a wealth of tryptamines, plus appendices presenting topics such as cactus alkaloids, natural betacarbolines, current drug law, and all known tryptamines that might be psychedelic. Once again the Shulgins honor us with an outstanding collection of vital information, particularly for those interested in the psychedelic field.

The Varieties of Psychedelic Experience. R.E.L. Masters and Jean Houston, Ph.D. Delta; 1966. A research-based comprehensive review of the effects of LSD on human personality, along with a section on the role and training of the guide.

BIBLIOGRAPHIES

The Albert Hofmann Collection: LSD & Psilocybin References
www.erowid.org

In the early 1950s, Sandoz began collecting LSD and psilocybin-related articles as part of Albert Hofmann's work with these substances. For nearly 35 years, Sandoz gathered over 4,000 documents: LSD and psilocybin journal articles from the late 1940s through the early-1980s, a few student theses, newspaper clippings, and other unique items. In the mid 1990s, the collection was given to the Albert Hofmann Foundation, and during the late 1990s, along with the Multidisciplinary Association for Psychedelic Studies and the Heffter Research Institute, they collaborated to create a digital index of the papers. In 2002, representatives from the Erowid web site and from MAPS completed the digital index of this entire collection.

Psycholytic and Psychedelic Research 1931-1995: A Complete International Bibliography. Torsten Passie, M.D., M.A., with preface by Hanscarl Leuner, M.D. Laurentius Publishers; 1997. To order contact MAPS by e-mail at askmaps@maps.org or contact Laurentius Publishers by e-mail at dehmlow@bib.mhhannover.de.

An excellent bibliography on the use of psychedelics in psychotherapy, this work is a valuable guide for students and researchers. A meticulous worldwide search by the author has revealed 687 pertinent scientific publications for further study. Research and therapeutic work with psychedelics remains controversial. The presentation of correct information helps overcome irrational projections, conclusions and prohibitions. Scientific research shows these catalysts can be used effectively and safely in medical psychotherapy.

This bibliography includes a precise subject index organized by substances, settings, methods, treatment results and more. The preface by Professor Hanscarl Leuner (Gottingen University, Germany), the leading European authority on research with psychedelics, provides an expert view. The introduction gives an overview of psycholytic and psychedelic therapy. This document is available as part of the Psychedelic Bibliography, at www.bibliography.maps.org

Religion and Psychoactive Sacraments: A Bibliographic Guide.
Thomas B. Roberts, Ph.D. and Paula Jo Hruby, Ed.D. (Eds.).

Contains over 550 annotated references to books and dissertations which address the topic of entheogens, psychoactive plants, and chemicals used within a religious context. In the view of editor Thomas Roberts, the *Guide* firmly establishes that theologians, clergy, scholars and laypersons see the topic of psychoactive sacraments as important and worthy of discussion and that disagreement, discussion, and debate exist over the questions: Is there legitimate religious use for psychoactive sacraments, and if so, what is appropriate? The index greatly enhances the usefulness of this booklet. Notes and Excerpts for each book range from half a page to three pages. The books described are almost exclusively in the English language and the emphasis is on North America. The editors note that the vast research in world-wide anthropology is under-represented and deserves a guide of its own. Available online at www.csp.org/chrestomathy.

Psychedelic Bibliography
www.bibliography.maps.org

This bibliography is designed to systematically digitize and protect the body of valuable psychedelic research papers for posterity. Sponsored by the Multidisciplinary Association for Psychedelic Studies, the Heffter Research Institute and the Albert Hofmann Foundation, this site mainly has annotated and non-annotated bibliographical listings but has some full-text listings. Includes bibliographies for: Psychedelics and the Dying; Psychedelics in Western Culture; Sandoz Pharmaceuticals' collection of research on LSD and psilocybin; Sasha Shulgin's MDMA bibliography; Howard Lotsof's ibogaine bibliography; the Janiger and Paltin bibliography of LSD.

By the same Author

Thanatos To Eros: Thirty-five Years of Psychedelic Exploration

Myron Stolaroff was the founder and President of the International Foundation for Advanced Study in Menlo Park, California, an organization devoted to research with LSD and mescaline from 1961 to 1965. Six professional papers covering this work have been published in appropriate journals.

Early on, Stolaroff was convinced of the value of psychedelic substances, and devoted his career to studying them. This book includes a detailed account of his own personal experiences coming to grips with an excruciatingly painful birth experience and its impact on his life, and learning to recognize and break free of powerful, oppressive feelings of failure and inadequacy. Facing and resolving repressed material opened the door to discovering the joy and vitality that life has to offer. It is a journey from the grip of Thanatos, the drive for death that effectively defeats enjoyment of life, to Eros, the drive for life that brings ultimate fulfillment.

An essential ingredient in the success of this struggle was the use of psychedelic substances. These sacraments, as he prefers to call them, allowed him to confront and resolve powerful shadow material. More important, they opened the gateway to that level of Divine love and grace that is the source of true healing and the freeing of our ultimate capacities.

Stolaroff's desire to discover effective means for self-realization led him to continue exploring newly discovered substances as long as they were legal. This book describes work done with family, friends, and research volunteers employing MDMA, 2C-B, 2C-T-2, 2C-T-7, 2C-E, and others. Numerous experiences are described in detail. Since for many people psychedelic experiences tend to fade if not appropriately utilized, serious consideration is given here to the concentrated effort required to accomplish rewarding changes.

These experiments and the discussions presented shed intriguing light on the nature of psychedelic experiences, the nature of the human psyche, factors affecting rewarding experiences, and aspects of transcendental levels of consciousness. Substantial evidence is presented of the inordinate power of the human mind, unrecognized by mainstream science-a power currently widely misdirected to create human pain and suffering. Numerous trials demonstrate that when used with integrity, skill, and fortitude, psychedelic substances can reveal the unfathomed love supporting all of creation, a love that can dissolve the death grip of Thanatos to free Eros and joyously illumine life in all of its aspects.

"I do not remember that a book from a living author impressed me more than *Thanatos to Eros*... My accord with your concepts of life and reality can best be summarized if I tell you that already in the first two paragraphs of the Introduction, the core of my belief has found its perfect, most beautiful expression."

—Albert Hofmann, Ph.D., retired Director of the Pharmaceutical Chemical Research Laboratories, Sandoz Ltd., Inventor of LSD

"Myron Stolaroff is one of the bravest, most sincere and forthright psychonauts of our time... The result is a book which speaks volumes to the psychology and spiritual worth of these substances..."

—Jon Hanna, *Psychedelic Resource List*

MAPS President Rick Doblin with Leo Zeff

About MAPS

HERE THERE BE DRAGONS

JUST 600 YEARS AGO, maps of the known world contained the inscription, "Here there be dragons," indicating *terra incognita* about which we knew nothing and hence feared to tread. Today we find this viewpoint exceedingly quaint. What changed? Knowledge and information was gathered by souls brave enough to challenge orthodoxy and venture into those uncharted realms inhabited by dragons. They returned with firsthand information that refuted "common knowledge" and led to a revised worldview.

Today, however, knowledge of our physical environment has expanded beyond belief.

Regarding our inner environment, however, many still fear that "here there be dragons." Replacing fear with understanding will require the use of every tool available, including psychedelic substances, to increase our knowledge of the internal terrain. Unfortunately, using psychedelics to explore these uncharted landscapes was forbidden for several decades.

However, in the last few years, a number brave scientists have been permitted to make the trek and conduct psychedelic research. Would you like to become part of this continuing "quest for knowledge?"

The Multidisciplinary Association for Psychedelic Studies (MAPS) was founded in 1986 as a 501 (c)(3) non-profit organization specializing in research and education that develops medical, legal, and cultural shifts which benefit the safe uses of psychedelics and marijuana for mental and spiritual healing. MAPS has dedicated over 35 years to changing the paradigm around how we think of, talk about, and consume psychedelics through research, education, and advocacy.

Printed in the USA
CPSIA information can be obtained
at www.ICGtesting.com
JSHW011542040324
58548JS00017B/386

9 798985 012217